NUMBER 436

THE ENGLISH EXPERIENCE

EXPERIENCE

ITS RECORD IN EARLY PRINTED BOOKS
PUBLISHED IN FACSIMILE

The publishers acknowledge their gratitude to the
Curators of the Bodleian Library, Oxford
for their permission to reproduce
the Library's copy, Shelfmark: 4°.A.43.Art.

Library of Congress Catalog Card Number:
71-38157

S.T.C.No. 3128
Collation: A-H^4 I^2

Published in 1972 by

Theatrvm Orbis Terrarvm Ltd.,
O.Z.Voorburgwal 85, Amsterdam

&

Da Capo Press Inc.
-a subsidiary of Plenum Publishing Corporation-
277 West 17th Street, New York N.Y. 10011

Printed in the Netherlands

ISBN 90 221 0436 2

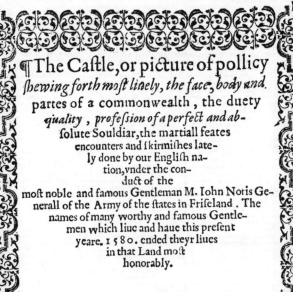

¶The Caſtle, or picture of pollicy
ſhewing forth moſt linely, the face, body and.
partes of a commonwealth, the duety
quality, profeſsion of a perfeȼt and ab-
ſolute Souldiar, the martiall feates
encounters and ſkirmiſhes lately done by our Engliſh nation, vnder the con-
duȼt of the
moſt noble and famous Gentleman M. Iohn Noris Generall of the Army of the ſtates in Friſeland . The
names of many worthy and famous Gentlemen which liue and haue this preſent
yeare. 1 5 8 0. ended theyr liues
in that Land moſt
honorably.

Handled in manner of a Dialogue betwixt
Gefferay Gate, and William Blandy,
Souldiars.

Faber eſt quiſque fortunæ ſuæ.

¶Anno 1 5 8 1 . .

¶AT LONDON
Printed by Iohn Daye, dwelling
ouer Alderſgate.

4ᵗ A. 43. Art.

TO THE NOBLE, AND
vertuous Gentleman M. Philipp SIDNEY.

WILLIAM BLANDY
Wisheth to his happy increase of knowledge,
the hoped and looked for fulnesse
of wisedome.

Ight Noble Sir (for what *letteth me to yelde you that title, sith your owne actions that I touch not herein your blood and Parentage whereof you are descended, may challenge as your especiall and proper right, the same) in my wandringes I found in an olde monument this written: I geue that, I haue not. Which Paradox or Riddle caused me to muse, with an earnest bent of my Imagination and iudgement, to the search and resolution, of so intricate and difficult a positiō. Laboring a long time (as in a labarinth) in the diuersity of sentences lōg sithens taught, deliuered, and receiued, I called at length to minde the verse of* Horrace.

Ego sum instar Cotis, acutum
Quæ reddat ferrum, tamen expers ipsa secandi.

And so perswading my selfe that it was ment of a whetstone, I took shortly in hand to play the whetstone my selfe: whetting and setting on edge (by this my slender and simple deuise) the blunt mindes of my countrymen, who are made able if they vsed wisely and a right the be-

A.ij.   nefite

The Epistle Dedicatorye.

nesite of Nature, to cut most deeply into those causes which
concerne the honor of our Prince, security and safegarde of
this commonwealth: most humbly praying you, who in my o-
pinion is able & sufficient to be both the whetstone and the
sword, I meane both to doe your selfe, and to moue and per-
swade other to all worthy & laudable actions, to take the
tuition of these my well meant labours and study.
The curteous & fauourable acceptatiō wher-
of, shall binde me euermore to be at your
becke, & happely stiri vp other of
more knowledge and dee-
per iudgement to the
attempt of some
greater good.

Desirous, (if it be in him) any
way to do you seruice.

WILLIAM BLANDY.

¶The copie of a letter sent by William Blandy , before the imprinting of his
booke , to his assured and worshipfull good
friend , *EDWARD MORRIS*,
Captayne.

ANIBALL exiled *Carthage*,
sought the supportance of *Antiochus* king of Ephesus . *Antiochus* embracing Chiualrye ,
would *Haniball* to be honored
of all his people : as one whose
worthye actes, and noble en-
terprises, filled at that tyme the
world with fame and glorye. This king, whether he
did therein respect his owne profite and wonted exercise, or pleasure and recreation of this valiant and
famous warriour , brought him to heare *Phormio*
reade, appoynted at that tyme to discourse of some
high poynt, and difficult question of Philosophie.
Antiochus and *Haniball* accompaned with many no-
bles, and braue courtiers of his nation , entred the
place of audience : *Phormio* laboring then no lesse in
the waightynes of his Argument, then a tall shipp
richly and heauely laden , tossed in the middest of
the Ocean . Whether the Maiestye of his king,
the coūtenaunce of so great,& honorable a person
as *Haniball* was , rushing in of so glittering and glori-
ous a troupe , or a vaine conceite of poore prayse
should moue in a deepe and approued Philosopher,
such chaungeablenes or no:*Phormio* suddaynely de-
clined from his intent and purpose, conuerting himselfe

selfe to the fpeach of warres . After whofe oration made and finifhed, *Antiochus* demaunded of *Haniball* what he thought of *Phormio* . I haue heard (fayd *Haniball*) many a Doter fpeake , but a more dreamer then *Phormio* is , fhall I neuer heare agayne . Which hiftory my good Captayne , is a prefident to me, (fith I write of the Martial affaires of our Country-men) to ftand in doubt , how this attempt of mine may be taken : for that there are emong our nation many *Haniballs*, but few of *Phormios* minde, & I, leaft able of all other, to fuftayne on my part, the waight of this cōparifon . My drift and defier therefore is, it would pleafe you to perufe thefe papers , and efpe-cially viewe that part, wherein is difclofed the pro-pertye , nature , and qualitye, of a good, and perfect Souldiar. Your will, or nill, fhall caufe me to follow or forfake my purpofe intended . My bufines , and being here in this land (as you know right well) is fuch, that I haue no long tarying. Where-fore returne I moft hartely pray you , as fpeedely as you may an Aunfwere. Fare you well.

Moft ready and willing
to pleafure you.

William

Blandy.

¶Edward Morris to his louing friend, *William Blandy.*

IPHICRATES THE ATHENIAN
Captayne , leading forth his Armye agaynſt
the Perſians , cauſed them to ſtay, to behold
the fighting of two Cockes . Which when
they had fought a long tyme , deliuered to
his Captaynes and Souldiars this manner
of ſpeach . Behold ſayd Iphicrates, the fight
of two ſeely foules , contending neither for
wife , nor chilàren, Countrye , libertye, glorye , houſe goodes , Church
goodes , nor holy thinges, but for onely victory . Much more ought wee
therefore (who are indued with a more excellent nature , and haue by
the inſtinct thereof, no leſſe care of wife , and children, libertye , fame
and victory , then of piety , and Religion of the Goddes) fight and
puiſſantly ſtand agaynſt the force and furye of the Enemy . If the example of Cock fighting , yelded to this noble Athenian Captaine , an
argument and reaſon, to prouoke and enkendle the mindes of his ſouldiars to prowes and valiantnes , who can iuſtly controlle your attempt
in this diſcourſe of warres : albeit I graunt you are in reſpect of an old
trayned Souldiar, but a very Cockerell. What I haue peruſed, my notes
and penne detecteth . Your endeuors cannot be but commendable,
deſart greater, if you were well employed . My good Blandy,
in concluſion , ſo farr is it , that I may call yonr ſtu-
dies into reprehenſion , that I could wiſhe other
your Elders in Militarie diſcipline, diſpoſed
as you are , and furniſhed with
your ſkill and facultye.

Your aſſured, and good
friend *Edward Morris.*

Lodowick Flood.

Might man ascend to see the sunne, to vewe the starres in skye:
 No doubt vnsweete the sight would be, might he not that discrye.
Thinges long desierd are sweete, thinges furre vnknowen are sought:
 Thinges secret seekes themselues to shewe, as nature them hath taught.
Where learning vttereth witt at will, and will to councell yeldes: (shield.
 There councell chargeth strength to stand, with sword, with speare and
Of no lesse prayse the penne in towne, then is the sword in field:
 For to the penne, as to the sword, ech Commonwealth must yeld.
A Castle calde of Pollicye, a glasse, a myrrour loe:
 Where nature first commendes the man, then Art the worke doth showe.
Where Mars doth fight with sword in hand, where Pallas pleades with quill:
 Where Neptune cutts the surging seas, where Ceres shewes her skill:
Here runnes the streames, here striues the states, here all are viewed with eye:
 Here triumphe sitts, here Trophes standes, here vertues throwne on hye.
The force of foes, the fence of friendes, the pathes of Pollicye playne:
 Where valiãt mindes, where worthy wightes, the crowne of fame may gaine
Sith Blandy seekes by Pollicye, his natiue soile to saue:
 Yeld due to Blandy worthy prayse, which Blandy ought to haue.
Some saucye Zoilous here will swell, some peeuish Pan will poute:
 Some fond Suffenus fault will finde, some carping Creete will doubt.
Alas poore man say some, and so in verdit passe
 How might he write of Pollicye, that Pollitick neuer was.
Can any make Mausolus toumbe, that Cetiphon did not viewe:
 Or who can frame a Labarinth, that neuer Dedalus knewe.
All coulours are not sitt nor fine, Alexanders shape to take:
 All kinde of woodes serues not the turne, Mercurius frame to make.
Who thinkes Gordius knot to vnknitt, must first with Phæbus talke:
 Who striues to fishe with Vulcans nett, he must to Cuma walke.
Tush, tush, his trueth, his trauell tryde, his care, his zeale you see:
 His fayth, his loue, his payne with penne, must here commended be.
Who in Treponius caue doth liue, shall with Cymmerians dye:
 Who drinkes of Letheus floud alway, the world shall him destroy.
Were it not report of prayse, of fame, of glory, of gayne:
 Fewe or none would warre or write, that could not prayse attayne.
Had Decius died as he had done, had Perseus ventured so:
 Had Theseus gone to Minotaure, had fame not bad him goe:
Had Hercules Cerberus sought in hell, had Iason gone from Greece:
 Had Cæsar Hasard sword and fier, had fame not fauored these:
The laborer lookes to haue his hier, the venturer hopes for gayne:
 The writer well may weare a Crowne, which euer shall remaine.
Sith fame doth sound the golden trumpe, and holdes the Crowne in hand:
 Let them approch to clayme the Crowne, which next to fame can stand.

FINIS.

Geffray Gate, William Blandy,
Speakers interchaungeably.

Ate. Syr, I am as glad of your safe
ariuall, as any one of your best, and
assured friendes.

Blandy. You had past by (I promise
you) vnknowen, had not your courtesie exceeded my memory. But now
that I call you to minde (my good
and approued friende) no man (be-
leue me) can be more welcome to me, then you, no man
more beloued of me, then your selfe : wherefore let not my
forgetfulnesse (I pray you) bring our friendshipp vnstey-
ned, so long and so deeply fixed, in question.

Gate. No feeblenesse of memory can purchase suspition,
or breede mislyke there, where inward affections ioyne,
and meete sweetely together: Sense, and feeling, is fraile
and slippery, what the minde recordeth, and caryeth in it
most faythfully imprinted, that I holde most deare and
pretious.

Blandy. Had I not alwayes noted in you that secret and excellent instinct, of the good and better vnderstanding: I had
neuer bene so much inclined towardes you.

Gate. I thanke you hartely of your good opinion, but
chiefely I ioy in this : that you and I agree in the onely
ground and foundation of true and perfect amitye, wherehence the causes of all noble actions whatsoeuer doe flowe:
that whatsoeuer we purpose, attempt, and aduenture, resteth wholy in the excellencye of the minde, and of that part
of the minde, which reason perswadeth, pietye directeth,
honor rewardeth, felicitye crowneth.

Blandy. What meane you syr, where you say of that part
of the minde ? Is not the minde a complete and entire
thing ? Is it not in his proper nature most pure, and free

in

The Caſtle of pollycye.

in it ſelfe from contagion? Oꝛ hauing moe partes, is there
a pꝛeheminence and ſuperioꝛitye?

Gate. The minde accoꝛding to the opinion of Philoſo-
phers (the true and diligent ſearchers out of naturall cauſes) is ſoꝛted twofoldly. The partition whereof, ſtandeth
chiefely of reaſon, then of ſence: the one hath leſſe, the other
moꝛe communion with the bodye. The reaſonable part in
euery well gouerned bodye, hath the dominion, and ruleth pꝛincipally. The duetye and action of the other, may
not vnfitly be compared (albeit in a contrary manner) to a
faythfull Coꝛpoꝛall, who diligẽtly attendeth the watch-
full, and carefull call of his Sentenell, oꝛ to a ready and
valiant ſouldiar, who executeth moſt ſpædely the will of
his commaunder. The office of the one, as of a chiefe, is to
commaunde, rule, and controlle: the dutye of the other to o-
bey, and cherefully pꝛoſecute the charge to him committed. So that as to an armye encamped no greater periil
can happẽ, if the Corporall ſlæpe, when the Sentenell calleth, oꝛ the Souldiar diſobey, whẽ the Chiefe, oꝛ Captayne
commaundeth: in lyke manner, a miſerable confuſion cannot but follow that minde and bodye, where right is abu-
ſed, and the courſe of nature violated.

Blandy. I cannot but aſſent (except I would ſtriue agaynſt
reaſon) to your good opinion. Foꝛ where fanſie is plan-
ted without iudgements appoynting, where luſt taketh
his pleaſure without reaſons lyking, where furye raun-
geth without politike direction, to conclude, where any
affect is found phantaſtick: there vnlooked foꝛ miſerie ouer-
takes the minde foꝛethinking, there ſoueraignetye lamen-
tably ſobbeth, thꝛough the ryott of indignitye.

Gate. I perceaue by your aſſertion, that euery man in
this lyfe (as on a Theatre oꝛ ſtage) playes one parte oꝛ o-
ther, which meriteth ſhame and obloquie, oꝛ deſerueth (as
his owne right) due commendation.

Blandy. It is an vndoubted veritye. O that men knew,
and

and dayly preſented before their eyes, the ſweete and glo=
rious garland that is purchaſed by vertue, and chiefely, by
Magnanimitye. There would not be then that vnſeaſo=
nable, and lothſome puffing, ſuch ſtrying, and wreſtling
would not be then for ſo vile a wretch. The complayntes
of the poore would not be then ſo many, and ſo pitifull, the
complayntes of the rich would not be found then ſo few
and beggarly. Gentlemen of great value, ſhould not then
wander as Pilgrims, in forrayne landes, ſuſpected as ba=
ſtardes, and children borne in haſt. Women of gentle
kinde & noble bloud, ſhould not be reputed as blaſted bloſ=
ſomes. O miſerye, O miſchiefe, O wickednes.

Gate. What tempeſt, what ſtyre, what tumult is this?
what curſed captiue is it you ſpeake of? wherehence pro=
ceedeth your woefull crye?

Blandy. I ſtand in doubt, whether ſilence were my beſt:
my minde notwithſtanding, indeuoreth to offend none,
moſt carefully willing my Countryes good.

Gate. I commend in no wiſe ſilence in him, whoſe minde
is ſo well bent, and diſpoſed: for his manner is to produce
good and fruitefull reaſon. wherefore ſay on, if you haue
conceaued aught, worthye the hearing.

Blandy. Being in Friſeland it was our happ (if you well
remember) wherein you tooke at that tyme no ſmall plea=
ſure, to be ofte rancked together: Where, partely to make
our labours more pleaſaunt, but chiefely to ſift and feele
ech others drift, you with many moe of ſound and ripe ex=
perience, moued queſtions to and fro of no ſmall vnpor=
tance. All which had relation to pollicye, and ciuile gouer=
ment.

Gate. I cannot eaſely forget the diuerſitie of thoſe diſcour=
ſes, interlaced with ſo many pleaſaunt and pithye ſpea=
ches. In ý varietye of which inuention, a caſtle by you ar=
tificially erected, was, of as many as heard your diſcourſe,
extolled to the ſkyes. wherein you (as ſome other Amphi-

on)moued, remoued, drewe, withdrewe the eares of your hearers, whither the progreſſe of your vnderſtanding (deliuered in ſo deyntye and trym wordes, in ſo decent and comely order, in ſo ſugred & ſwæte a tongue) bent it ſelfe. Wherefore recount, I moſt hartely pray you the ſame agayne.

Blandy. I thinke it not beſt.

Gate. Why ſo I pray you?

Blan. Were it not (thinke you) a poynt in me of great follye & raſhneſſe, to committ to the viewe of wiſe and learned men a repetition of a weariſome tale and fond Imagination, eſpecially knowing my ſelfe to haue receaued the leaſt portion of learning, wherewith infinite nūbers of our owne Countrymen and ſtraũgers are plentifully indued? Agayne, what fruite will you reape, or who will the more accompt of vs, if you and I ſpeake, or write of knowledge, in a worlde replete and glutted with letters? Farther who will now almoſt looke vpon, and regard any inuention, except it ſenteth lyke a flower, and in ſhew, and hue be lyke vnto a Lillye? Laſtly, doe not you hazard greatly your credite, to ioyne with ſo poore and ſimple a man, any way as my ſelfe, you being through many daungerous and bitter bruntes, in the field approued, in Martiall affaires expert, for your ſkill and pollicye reputed?

Gate. *Diſcreete and ſober men pardone imperfection, where the minde and inclination is good. The fruite that I purpoſe, and hope hereby to reape, is the weale of my Countrye. Which honeſt and vpright intent, thowſand moe writers can no wiſe preiudice. And whereas many fauor pleaſures, and therefore couet ſuch letters, which you haue not vnproperly compared to* flowers,& Lillyes *(which by nature are good, yelding a ſweete but yet a ſhorte ſent, pleaſing rather the ſence of ſome ſingular perſons, then profiting the ſoule of a Commonwealth) yet all are not ſo ledd and minded. Wherefore vnto thoſe other, theſe labors ſhall be dedicated, who are of a more highe and lofty ſpirite: your pouertye which you meane, and ſpeake of, hindreth*
not

not, but that you may be much more, for that inricht in minde.
Simplicity is the ground and roote of heauēly wiſedome. In con-
cluſion who could fitt me to addreſſe and finiſh this good and ho-
neſt enterpriſe ſo well as he, that hath bene my fellow Souldiar in
the warres, who hath alſo (except I be deceaued greatly) more
then taſted of the ſtreames and riuers of learning? Wherefoꝛe
be of gꝺd courage, my powers are pꝛeſt to vpholde your
penne.

Blādy. I am altogether wonne to your gꝺd deſire: building
my laboꝛs (as on a ſure & vnmoueable rock) vpō your dꝛep
and tryed iudgement. Yet ſo, that we both ſubmitt whatſoeuer ſhall be by vs vttered, to the verdite and cenſure of
thoſe who pꝛeuaple in witte, ercell in knowledge and learning. The abſolute frame and building therefoꝛe, whereof
I in our March diſcourſed, conſiſted of ſire Romes and
Chambers.

Gate. Befoꝛe you enter further into this diſcourſe, ſhew
me (I pꝛay you) the foꝛme and figure of the frame.

Blandy. It was ſphericall, oꝛ round.

Gate. How were the lodginges deuided?

Blandy. The Rꝏfe and higheſt couering conteyned thꝛꝺe
eſpeciall Chambers with theyꝛ peculiar offices, directly vn-
derneath were other thꝛꝺe by ſquares and ſpaces diſtinc-
ted. And to the end you ſhould holde it to be the onely monument in the woꝛlde, (beleue me) the rareſt Mathemati-
tian in Europe, vewed firſt the place and accoꝛding to the
ſwꝺte and ſafe conſtillation of the ſtarres dꝛew the Platt:
deliuering to poſterity this teſtimony foꝛ his perpetuall
honoꝛ and memoꝛy, ẏ if the partes within did alwayes ob-
ſerue and aunſwere the face of the frame, they ſhould feare
no foꝛce, no fury, no bꝛauado, no bullett, no battery.

Gate. The figure of this frame is ſo abſolute, the ſtate-
lineſſe ſo ſumptuous, the beauty ſo ſꝺmely and ercꝺding
rich, that I may dꝺme it, foꝛ right gꝺd cauſe, the onely pa-
terne and pꝺreles Pallace in ẏ woꝛld, what name hath it?

Blandy. This Architecture hight Pollicye.

Gate. For whome was this fumptuous and curious worke wrought, who fhall poffeffe a Pallace fo pœreles?

Blandy. A King, A Iufticer, A Souldiar, A Marchaunt, An Artificer, A Tiller of the ground.

Gate. Are thefe the partes you fpake of before? is this the power that fhall poffeffe and defend with fecurity thys inuincible forte? May no one of greater fkill and dœper reatch controle this diuifion, adde vnto, or diminifh the number?

Blandy. In no wife.

Gate. Why fo?

Blandy. The workemanfhip is fo rare, the ftrength wher-of ftandeth on the combination of the partes within contayned.

Gate. What is that? of what kinde and excellency is it, that hath fo faft glued them together, and is to the frame fo great a ftay and firmament?

Blandy. I will fhew you. To every parte before rehear-fed, belonges his proper and peculiar vertue and qualitye. To the Prince, preheminence, to the Iufticer, iudgement, to the Souldiar, puiffaunce, to the Marchaunt, defire to be enriched, to the Artificer, delight in his occupation, to the Tiller of the groud, true obedience. That which doth moft firmely and ftrogly ioyne and knitt thefe partes together, is Proportion: which broken and defaced, not onely ren-teth and plucketh in funder the frame, but tottereth with-all, and tumbleth down the Prince, peruerteth iuftice, poy-foneth and plucketh downe the good and vpright minde of the Souldiar, robbeth the Marchaunt, ranfacketh the Ar-tificer, fpoyleth vtterly the fimple and poore labourfome man.

Gate. Is this that you call Proportion, a thing of fo great perfection?

Blandy. Proportion is of that force and ftretcheth forth fo
largely

largely,that no mã without an especiall regard of it,can well go-uerne himselfe:in a Family,Citty,and commõ wealth, the power thereof doth more eminently appeare.

Gate.　*What is Proportion(I pray you)shew me?*

Blandy.　Proportion is the iust , right,and naturall meafure of thinges , directed to theyr originall and first creatiõ . So that what foeuer is moze,oz leſſe,greater,oz ſmaller, then Arte hath deuiſed, ꝛ courſe of kinde kept ꝛ obſerued in all ages, limited to the firſt and ſucceſſiue ſhape, not onely of men, but of all other thinges created , is in no wiſe to be called propoztioned.

Gate.　When all thinges haue accozding to your opinion, a right oz wzong,a iuſt oz vniuſt propoztion.

Blandy. In no wiſe ſo. Foz this opinion I defend that all thinges propoztioned are ſtraightened and made vpzight thzough knowledge and wiſedome : all other crooked and miſhapen thinges are to be termed Monſters , not adding thereunto the name of propoztion:foz that they are made ꝛ ingendzed thzough errozand blindeneſſe.

Gate.　If you would in a ſimile oz example moze playnely diſcloſe your dzifte , you ſhould doe me a right acceptable pleaſure.

*Blandy.　*As there is in the body a fayze oz foule, a neate oz leſſe fine,an amiable oz odible feature,that is,when euery part accozding to his accuſtomed and naturall propoztion aunſwereth other, oz as ſuperfluous lumpes reſulteth:So there is in the minde(betwixt which,in excellency and cre-ation of nature there is no compariſõ) a dimme oz daynty, a cleare oz cloudy, a rough oz royall , a harde oz gentle and haughty Image,foz both which,accozding to their vnſeme-ly oz ſweete,cleane oz cozrupt ſtate,ſome are lothed , ſome ſoued, ſome refuſed , other rapſed to honoz and dignity. Whoſe heele exceeds his head in quatity,whoſe arme ſwel eth,and hath in it as it were a blowing billow as bigge as his waſt , we (not reckoning ſo much of his miſerye and

wꝛetchedneſſe, wherewith he is moſt pittifully wꝛapt in)
ſcarſe number him (and that foꝛ right good cauſe) among
men. In like maner, in whoſe minde there is an intruſion
made, that is where luſtfull pleaſure, fond fancye, wilfull
deſire, taketh reaſon with all her powers and faculties pꝛi-
ſoners, and bꝛing them in moſt lamentable and mourning
maner like Captiues faſt chayned to the lothſome & darcke
dungeon of ſcilence: there the excellencye of Pꝛopoꝛtion
in that part is as much euerted, as if the earth ſhould become no moꝛe ẙ Centre, & violently contrary to kinde challenge the chiefe and ſuperioꝛity of fire, and fire, contrary to
all reaſon, fall downe and vpholde the water.

Gate. Your reaſon reſoundeth their ſaying who affirme,
that no coꝛrupt, can ſuppꝛeſſe a finer creature.

Blandy. Me thinkes, as they iudge: howbeit ſometimes ca-
ſually oꝛ rather by the ſufferance of God, the earth and water contayneth an aiery part: which notwithſtanding, in
thoſe lower caues and dennes beneath, in his kinde ſtri-
ueth moſt egerly, and at length bꝛeaketh out to the terroꝛ
and amaſing of men: flying (as one redœmed out of thꝛall)
vp agayne to his wonted place of reſt. So that euery thing
diſoꝛdered, commeth either to ineuitable loſſe and ruine,
by the extremitye of riott, oꝛ by natures good grace & go-
uermēt, receaueth againe his accuſtomed light and beauty.

Gate. You haue to my thincking done well.

Blandy. If what I haue ſayd, be to any auaileable, it ſhall
pleaſe me right well to receaue the ſame (as from a cleare
and changeable welſpꝛing) of your owne lipps againe,
wherefoꝛe, repeate (foꝛ the ſingular loue you beare me)
bꝛiefely what I haue diſcloſed.

Gate. You haue ſpoken of the minde and bodye: betwixt
the beautye & defoꝛmitye whereof (as you haue declared)
there is no compariſon. Foꝛ I holde the calamitie of that
minde and bodye incomparable, were the outward partes
neuer ſo vnpꝛoper, the pearcing eye of whoſe minde ſenſe

hath

hath blered , whofe gliftring lookes luft hath obfcured , the
light of whofe vnderftanding and memozy , erroz fpzin-
ging of earthlynes , hath ouerwhelmed with palpable
darcknefle.

Blandy. Pou rehearfe nothing els, but whereunto I moft
willingly affent.

Gate. Pou haue moft friendly fatiffied the moyetye of
my demaunde , the other bzaunche , whereof I fhall taft
fome finer fruite , I defier with zeale to fee it fpzead fozth.

Blandy. What part and bzaunch is that?

Gate. Pou haue fpoken of the defozmitye of the minde ,
Now it is conuenient you tell vs of a confozmed minde,
oz (as you pleafe) of a minde pzopoztioned: that the feeme-
ly fhape thereof being knowen , might enamour vs with
the grace and bzauery of her beautye .

Blandy. When I confider the wonderfull greatnes , and
wozthynes of the minde , garnifhed with all pzetious
gemmes of noble vertues, I finde no flozifh of eloquence,
no lights of learning, no trym fpeaches , oz Rhetozicall
wozdes fufficient foz his defcription . Foz if the fharpe
witts of thofe who haue pzofeffed Eloquence , when
they would defcribe the pzayfes of any humaine vertue,
were with the waight of the matter fometimes fo cloyed,
that their fenfes (to theyz great fhame and rebuke) were
cleane ouerwhelmed : how much moze ought I then poze
feely and fimple man, ftay & ftagger, fearing, foltring, dzea-
ding to be dzowned (as in a deepe lake) in fo ample highe
and graue an argument.

Gate. I commend truely herein moze your modefty, then
courage and wifedome . Foz I holde this the pzoperty of a
well difpofed, and good natured young man, earneftly bent
in the ftudye of moft wozthye knowledges, not to reft contented with thinges of meane account, but earneftly pzofe-
cute and clime vnto the higheft caufes : and then to be-
ftirre himfelfe, and laboz feruently, when he feeth himfelfe

C.j.   to be

to be intangled with greateſt difficulty. Wherefoꝛe albeit
you are in your owne opinion, (by reaſon of any witt and
ererciſe)able litle to do, ſæing that you haue taken in hand
ſo great and difficult a matter, I holde your blame in ge⸗
uing ouer.greater,then boldeneſſe in taking it in hand.

Blandy. Your perſuaſion,(ſith what you haue ſayd is true)
hath wonne me altogether: and the rather, that the action
is right good and honeſt.Wherefoꝛe I am addꝛeſſed (as my
pœꝛe ability will ſerue) to diſcourſe largely of the ercellen⸗
cy of the minde,and his creation.

Gate. Say on,I ſhall bend and recline my eare diligētly.

Blandy. The moſt ercellent power and maieſty of that hea⸗
uenly minde,which being moſt high and euerlaſting, we
woꝛthely reuerence and adoꝛe as our God, as the euerla⸗
ſting fountayne of life, as the maker and creatoꝛ of all
thinges, when it did ſæme good to his bnſpeakeable wiſe⸗
dome,to deale bountifully, imparting his benefites to ma⸗
ny(foꝛ nothing ſheweth ſo much the goodneſſe and bertue
of God as his fræ beneficence) in the beginning he created
the inuiſible woꝛld,beautified with holy Aungels,who be⸗
holding alwayes his incompꝛehenſible light and bꝛightnes
doe liue in euerlaſting bleſſedneſſe.

Gate. Came all thoſe his creatures to the ſame eſtate of
gloꝛy and immoꝛtality?

Blandy. In no wiſe. Thoſe onely enioyed that pleaſaunt
plott of infinite reſt, who repoſed the ſtay and Caſtle of
their ſafety, the lightnes of their bꝛightnes, the cauſe and
end of theyꝛ bleſſed life,in theyꝛ Loꝛd and maker.

Gate. Did any of thoſe holy and heauenly wightes fall
from the true honoꝛ of theyꝛ creatoꝛ?

Blandy. Holy ſcripture learneth bs of an infinite number,
the chiefe of whom was named Lucifer.

Gate. What was theyꝛ impiety(I pꝛay you ſhew) decla⸗
ring withall theyꝛ puniſhment?

Blandy. Theſe ſirſt fell to ẏ neglect ɛ contempt of God,
being

being enamozed with the beauty of themſelues, and main-
tayning ſtill this rebellious ſpirit: yelded at length to they-
owne natures a kinde of pzeheminence in glozy, not vn-
like to the very Godhead. Wherſfoze they were depziued
of that paſſing cleare light, whereof they were moſt vnwoz-
thy, and thzowne downe into the place of perpetuall and
euerlaſting miſery, and into the darcke dungeon of that
night that ſhall euer continue. So that after God had made
the higheſt heauens and wonderfull wozke thereof, which
no eye hath ſæne, then he framed this wozld moſt beauti-
fulland of exceding fayzeneſſe, garniſhing it with all pleaſures and commodities. In the making whereof he vſed no
other engine oz deuiſe then his owne will and pleaſure.

Gate. To what purpoſe, and foz whoſe vſe that moſt high
creatoz and Lozd of all thinges hath made this ſo beautiful
wozkemanſhipp, this ſo excellent fozme and ſhape of heauenly bodies, this ſo large and ſpacious greatneſſe of ſea
and land? Foz it is not the pzactiſe of his infinite wiſedome
to doe any thing in vayne, but foz ſome excellent ende and
purpoſe. Foz whoſe ſake then, did (he after a moſt wonderfull ozder) frame that moſt godly and ſæmely ſubſtance of
thinges, diſlike in nature, and yet agræing among themſelues? Foz his owne ſake thinke you, becauſe he would
haue a trimmer habitation?

Blandy. In no wiſe, Foz it were not onely a wicked thing,
but a poynt of extreame madneſſe, to thinke ſo of that moſt
bleſſed minde, then the which nothing moze perfect and abſolute may be imagined: the vertue and power whereof is
infinite and inſcrutable, to haue næded any earthly and bo-
dily tabernacle, oz that at all times befoze he wanted ſome-
what to accompliſhing of perfect bleſſedneſſe, oz to the fulnes of his glozy, oz that God coulde be encloſed within any
certayne rome oz compaſſe.

Gate. What then? were theſe thinges pzouided foz the
Aungels and Saintes of God?

Blandy In no wiſe. Foz they being ſeuered, and fræ from

all fellowſhipp and coniunction of the bodye, deſire nothing els but to behold their maker , neither can they reape any commoditye, o2 conceaue any pleaſure of thinges beneath in theſe lower partes. And to thinke this great and wonderfull wo2ke to be made fo2 vnreaſonable creatures, o2 fo2 the vſe of trees and plantes , fo2 fiſhes , by2des ,and fowles,it were to to abſurde. God hath not therefo2e deuiſed this ſo goodly and beautifull a frame fo2 himſelfe , fo2 Aungels,fo2 the fruites of the earth , fo2 creatures voyde of reaſon, but fo2 man.

Gate. In all this ſeaſon , where was man , fo2 whome God had p2epared ſo beautifull, ſo rich , ſo bountifull a kingdome?

Blandy. *Man was in the minde ,vertue, and iudgement of God.* So that , when at length the wo2ld it ſelfe was finiſhed, he made firſt a bodye of earth, thẽ he b2eathed therein a minde finely faſhioned, acco2ding to his owne Image and ſimilitude. Sy2 ſee you not manifeſtly the beginning and creation of the moſt excellent and noble minde of man?

Gate. I behold it (as in a glaſſe) deriued and taken out from no other thing, then the ſpirite of God: and being incloſed in the bodye (as in a wo2thy beſſell) retaineth a deuine fo2me , pure, and deuoyd of all filthy co2ruption.

Blan. This was (I aſſure you) mans firſt eſtate, this was the firſt beginning & foundation of that excellencye whereunto man aſpired , wherein no man can note any thing, but that which is right hono2able , and wo2thye of high eſtimation. Then the bodye was not infected with any vice, whereby reaſon might be diſturbed, o2 the minde obſcured with darcknes. Man knewe then, all ſciences , vnderſtœde the cauſes of all thinges, was ſufficiently learned in the rule and diſcipline of lyfe, being inſtructed by no other teacher thẽ God himſelfe, the geuer of all knowledge and wiſedome . And he did not onely excell all other creatures in the comely ſhape and feature of his bodye , but he

was

was farr beyond them all in the amiable, most excellent, and deuine forme and figure of the minde. For there was in the minde no error, no motion in the sence, whereby the rule of reason might be disordered: whereas reasō it selfe, as it were in a perfect and florishing Commonwealth, so in a peaceable and quiet estate, could very easely restraine all raging affections. The minde therefore had no kinde of lett and impediment, whereby it might be hindered from dayly contemplation.

Gate. As your speach hath in a manner surprised me with ioy, to thinke of our originall, to call to memory, how gratiously the power of the almighty, dealt with vs (and to speake the vttermost) that we proceded from the nature and substaunce of God him selfe: so I feele out of measure a touch of griefe, when I consider that we remaine not in the estate of our former felicitye, the chopse so happy, the chaunge being so lamentable. Wherefore, open (I pray you) the cause of so greuous and great a calamitye.

Blandy. After God had shewed himselfe so liberall, & boutifull towardes man, he made him president and chiefe ruler of the earth, appoynting him a princely place for his habitation. The *Greekes* call it *Paradice* : *a Garden flowing with most pleasaunt and siluerlyke springes, most delectable, and decked with greate store aud varietye of sweete senting flowers, most fitt to liue in all felicitye and pleasure*. In this most pleasaunt seate, Man was placed, that by that place, (which as some say) was high, & moūted aloft, he mought learne not onely lyke a ruler and gouernour, wisely to guide the sterne thereof: but also thereby be admonished w discrete gouernement and free libertye, to take vpon him the charge and rule ouer all other liuing creatures. He had therefore a princely iurisdiction ouer earth, he serued onely the Lord of heauen, and being a holy one, wholy dedicated to God, he was the expounder of his holy will and pleasure, and the chiefe Prince, and first parent of all man-

kinde

kinde. He had a lawe geuen him, that he should exercise
that free will in the practise of vertue, that at length he
might by his owne demerites, deserue to be of the number
and company of heauenly Saintes. And the law was, that
he should not presume to touch the fruite of a certayne ex-
céeding goodly apple trée, which conteyned the knowledge
of good and euill.

Gate. Did God geue him this commaundement, that he
disdayned, that man whome he had manifoldly blessed,
should haue no vnderstanding thereof?

Blandy. In no wise: but that by that meanes he would the
better forefee and prouide for those thinges which apper-
teyned to his good estate and preseruation. For he knew
right well, that if man were set at libertye, he would
straight way worke his owne confusion. So therefore, God
did moderate his libertye, by ordayning that necessary and
expedient lawe. Neither did he so much forbid him to eate
of that fruite, as that he should not slipp into that, which
by that fruite was meant and signified.

Gate. I could neuer yet heare, or haue imagined any other
meaning thereof, then the letter testifieth.

Blandy. Whether this may be construed of the not eating
of the fruite or no, I leaue it, and stand to the iudgement
and correction of other: that is, that he should not meddle
with those causes, or search by his owne industrye to attayne the knowledge of those thinges, which his capacitye
could not reach and comprise: Or that he should not in the
choyse of good, and refusall of the euill, vse rather his owne
iudgement, then the will and pleasure of the Almightye,
by whose wisedome he should yelde himselfe to be gouerned: Or this, that he should not incline himselfe to the
loue of those good thinges which are mixt and intermedled
with a number of euills: therefore I say, whether he gaue
that commaundement to Man, that he embracing that so-
ueraigne good, that is not intermedled with any enill,
                                                    should

should vtterly refuse other good things which appeare faire
and pleasaunt, and yet are corrupt and poysoned : what
more wholesome precept and comaundement might haue
bene ordayned more profitable for Man.

Gate. Your saying is most true . For our wittes are vt=
terly confounded , and cloyed with the search of those cau=
ses, the exceeding deepnes whereof our capacity may not be
able to compasse, *& in any affayres, to follow our owne braine,
and not to be ledd by the light of the wisedome of God, it is a
most vndoubted token of our fall and vtter confusion.*But to be
leadd away from that good thing which is most principall
and the onely piller and firmament that holdeth vp this pro
portioned minde you speake of , being deceiued with the
sweetenesse of any vayne and transitory pleasure, it is to be
holden generally a thing most daungerous and deadly.

Blandy. This therefore was the estate of our first parent
which should haue bene most happy and blessed , if he had
not acquaynted himselfe with that huge and cruell mon=
strous beast, y hath brought to all nations pestilent infecti=
ons. For when the Prince of darckenesse (the chiefe Cap=
taine of those Angels as I haue declared) who through the
puffe of Pride fell into the lamentable and pittifull pitt of
perdition, who vnderstood and saw man made of earth, as=
cend into that place of glory fro whence he fell: he through
mallice waxed hoate , imagining all kinde of meanes to o=
uerthrow vtterly the state of mankinde. Taking vpon him
theretore the shape of a Serpent assaulted through guiles
and fayned sleightes, the woman our first parentes fellow
mate, whom he thought to subdue with lesse labor, for that
she was frayle and the feebler vessell, he therefore inticeth
her, and with sweete and sugred wordes allureth her , to
the eating the fruit forbidden: bearing her in hand, that as
soone as she should take a tast of that most pleasaunt Ap=
ple, she should eftsoone be inspired with that heauenly know=
ledge, of good and euill. The woman therefore being mar=

C.iiij.   ueilously

neiloufly allured with the fayzeneſſe of the trée,and alſo inflamed aboue meaſure with the deſire of that heauenly ſcience and wiſedome,was eaſily induced to dzinke that cupp
of deadly popſon, offered vnto her , by that moſt ſubtle and
peſtilent Serpent. Thus,the woman neglecting the commaundement of the moſt high God , and gracious geuer of
all goodneſſe,folowed the counſell of her moſt deadly enemy,inuiting alſo her huſband to that woefull and bloudye
banquett. *This was the originall and beginning of the miſery of*
man . Herehence came all troubleſome motions of minde,here-
by was ingédred in the fleſh all chaũgeable & wauering deſires,
herehence came all kinde of corruption , herehence ſprang all
fooliſh and vayne opinions : from this roote roſe mortality,moſt
bitter and greuous lamentations, ſorrowes, ſobbes , and grones,
for feare of death grew from this foundation : which the ſæly
and wzetched minde of man incontinently felt . Foz this
was moſt iuſtly decréed,that he which had bzoken the commaundement of his Lozd,and moſt impudently and wic-
kedly ſtood agaynſt his will and pleaſure , in like manner
ſhould haue thoſe parts which befoze were obedient, rebellious and contrarply diſpoſed,aſſaying moſt deſperately to
inuade and ouerthzow the foztreſſe of reaſon. And whereas
two thinges eſpecially belonged to man , that is to exerciſe himſelfe in action and cõtemplation,and therefoze was
indued with a reaſonable minde , that in whatſoeuer he
tooke in hand, he ſhould wiſely gouerne euery affect of the
minde and imploy all the power of his minde in ſearching
out of heauenly wiſedome : he in both theſe partes was
dæpely wounded . Foz the minde, when the cleare light
therof was extinct,wherewith it befoze gliſtred glozioufly,
lay now ouercaſt with darckeneſſe and obſcurity , and the
whole ozder of life being(as it were with darcke night) o-
uerwhelmed , was wellnigh put beſide his rule and ſoue-
raygnety,ſo that although in that darckeneſſe ſome glimſe
of light appeared, yet could it not thereby be guyded to the
                                                              end

and deſired. Then ſhamefull filthyneſſe ſhewed it ſelfe, be¬
fo2e that time bnknowen, by the ougly ſight and monſtru¬
ous aſpect whereof,our firſt partes being diſmayed,ſh2ow¬
ded theſelues in darcke woodes , and couered thoſe partes
with leaues of trees , which they felt to be moſt ſtriuing a¬
gaynſt reaſon and bnderſtanding . Nothing was done in
thoſe dayes fo2 a great ſeaſon by due o2der of reaſon and di¬
ſcipline , but all matters were executed biolently whereas
frantique and furious headineſſe had the bpper had. Then
Robberyes were rife,then rapes common , then inceſt not
accompted of, then murthers infinite. Then thoſe , who in
fo2ce and ſturdines paſt other , tooke it no offence at their
pleaſure to afflict & puniſh the weaker ſo2t . In this great
darknes, in this common miſerye, in this bniuerſall woe¬
fulnes, there appeared a man,who th2ough his cleane and
bnſpotted handes, his cleare & pityfull eyes , his ſtreight
and bp2ight minde,d2ewe many extremely handled, to his
reuerence,loue,and hono2. Whome when they noted, not
onely to abſteine himſelfe from billany , but bend to Cap¬
tiues and Murtherers a ſterne and irefull countenaunce,
and take commiſeration of the afflicted : then theſe w2et¬
ched wo2mes crawled bnto him , making a ſcritch & woe¬
full cry . Of whoſe ſutes and lamentable complayntes ,
when he had taken compaſſion , and ſought by witt and
pollicie to ayde and aſſiſt, became bnto them at length , a
lanterne of Juſtice , a mirrour of mildnes and courteſie .
This ſuppo2ter of right , when he had taken on him the
charge of thoſe ſelye ſoules miſerably , and ſupplyantly
yealding theinſelues to his o2der and direction : and decla¬
red bnto them the earneſt deſier he had to take away all in¬
iurious inuaſions , and to rep2eſſe biolent murthers , and
baliantly to reuenge w2ongfull opp2eſſions, and to linke
bnder lyke lawes, both the mighty men and ſimpler ſo2te:
it came to paſſe , that as many as tendered their peculiar
libertye, and ſought their owne ſecuritye and quietnes,

ſuppo¬

supposed him to be the defence and bulwarke of their safe and prosperous estate, whose fame most florished for iustice and equitye. Behold here (my good friend) the fountayne and head spring, from whence hath flowed the power and authoritye of kinges, the preheminence, and prerogatiue of princely gouernment. Herehence soueraigntye, and the cause of all renowne and glory was deriued.

Gate. I perceaue by your discourse, y the originall, from whence hath issued this high and stately gouernement of Kinges, is worthy all reuerence, honor, and obedience: and that there is no one stock more auncient, or more excellent, then the *Petegree of Princes*, which through their owne vertue and valiantnes abandoned all barbarous crueltye, reducing the people to good order and ciuilitye.

Blandy. You see therefore manifestly how Principalitye grewe first, and that equitye and puissance were the rootes and raysers of royaltie, and that no king can holde long his scepter sure, if his minde become base through vniustice and dastardly feare.

Gate. Doe these two vertues onely make in a Prince the fulnes of a florishing fame? needeth the *Maiestye of a King* no more, for the setting forth of his glistring and shyning glorye?

Blandy. There are other twoe most necessary, which also must accompany the other spoken of before, as speciall and chiefe vertues.

Gate. What name haue they?

Blandy. The one is called Prudence, the other Temperaunce.

Gate. If you would more at large, display their singular condicions, and priuate natures, you should doe me a right acceptable friendshipp, & percase your report should bring no small profite to many other of the simpler sort.

Blandy. No will (I assure you) shall want in me, to pleasure you, or profite any, reckoning my selfe most fortunate, if the meanest man may reape of my penn the

least

leaft fruite,

Gate. Pou fpeake moft friendly , wherefoze I hartely pzay you, fay on.

Blandy The excellencie therefoze of iuftice,ftands of fozce, and vertue: the vertue of iuftice refteth in the meafure of thinges ozdered, accozding to reafons pzefcription , which teacheth that all men fhould beare the lyke affection to other,as they would be affected of other. The fozce of iuftice is to make of many, one, fo vnite and knit many partes in one : which euidently may appeare, if we call to minde that in the beginning it did fo greatly excite and ftirre vp mens mindes, that foz her loue they furrédered their goods and poffeffions into the handes of one efpeciall man , in whofe amiable face this vertue did thzough flafhing flames fhewe fozth her cleare light of glozy . I reade of Numa Pompilius a Romaine of meane eftate , who by vpzight dealing,and fuppozting of Juftice , was thought and pzo- clapmed by the whole confent of the Romaines , woxthe- ly to fuccéde Romulus in the ftate of Royall Maieftye. What needeth me here to fpeake of Licurgus,Draco, and *Solon,* that I omit in meane while to make mention of Mercurie, Phoroneus , Pittacus of Millen , and diuers other , who by iuftice haue bene aduaunced to great honoz, and haue thereby purchafed to their pofteritye, perpetuall fame and memozye . Therefoze, to perfwade our felues that no one vertue deferueth the lyke pzeheminéce, cyther is alyke to be honozed, it is hereby to be féene , that each kinde of vertue being voyde of Juftice, hath loft his honoz and eftimation , whereas *Iuftice alone fecluded from other vertues,retayneth ftill his efpeciall grace & dignitie.*Where- by it is euident and playne , that there is no way moze cer- cayne then this , to enlarge our honoz, no way moze readilye to commend to pofteritye our fame and memo- rye.

Gate. I reft fatiffied with your not fo fhozt as fwéete

diſcourſe. It remaineth that you ſpeake of foꝛtitude.

Blandy. Fortitude reſteth in an inuincible minde, attempting for the loue of ſome excellent thing, great, difficult, and daungerous actions. Which high and lofty courage hath bene in all ages woꝛthely magnified. *For it is a matter of no ſmall importance, ſo litle to eſteeme of lyfe, (which we all in generall deeme to be ſweete)as to beſtow it willingly, and cherefully for the ſafegard and preſeruation of a fewe, and to refuſe and feare for the wealth of our Countrie no daunger and terror of the enemy.* The recoꝛdes and oꝛdinaunces of antiquitye, doe playnely and manifeſtly ſhewe, that there hath bene no gloꝛye ſo great, no renowme ſo honoꝛable in any well gouerned Commonwealth, as that which hath bene attributed to valiantnes and foꝛtitude. On the other ſide there were foꝛ Cowards euē by very good lawes, bitter tauntes and repꝛoches, moſt iuſtly appoynted. *There was in olde tyme among the Macedonians a lawe ordeyned, that he who had not in fight of battaile ouercome one, ſhould in the ſight of all men be truſt vp with an halter.* Therefoꝛe, moſt wiſely was it thought of Solō greatly honored among the Grecians for his deepe iudgement, that the ſecuritye and pꝛeſeruatiō of a Commonwealth, did conſiſt in pꝛeferment, & puniſhmēt. Foꝛ by this, wicked and deſperate perſons are reſtrained & cut of, by the other, noble natures & floꝛiſhing witts are vehemētly ſtyꝛred vp to ẏ embꝛacing of vertue & honeſtye. It hath bene therefoꝛe by deuine pꝛouidence eſtabliſhed of our foꝛefathers, ẏ in what kinde of men ſocuer this vertue eminently appeared, the ſame ſhould be with many woꝛthye and noble enſignes, and titles honoꝛed. And that I ſpeake ſomething of the Romaines, *Can any man be able to recite ſo many Images of men of Armes, So many garlands either geuen to them that ſcaled the walles, or firſt entred their enemies Tents, or to them that by maine force ſaued the life of any one Citizen, or to them, that victoriouſly triumphed ouer their enemies?* Is any man able to recompt ſo many
enſignes

enſignes of vertue,ſo many pꝛyſes of Pꝛayes,as to pꝛowes
and puiſſaunce were by the Romaine lawes aſſigned?
Gate. It is not therefoꝛe to be maruailed at,that that Cit-
tie grewe to be ſo great and large in Empire, wherein
pꝛowes and baliantnes was ſo honoꝛably rewarded.
Blan. In that people, this is alſo greatly to be noted , that
not onely noble men were wonderfully inflamed with the
loue of gloꝛye, but very many of the common people . And
that I may, of a great and infinite number , call a fewe to
memoꝛy , the two Decii by race and byꝛth no gentlemen,
foꝛ theyꝛ rare and ſingular foꝛtitude,aſpired in the commõ
wealth to the higheſt degrée of honoꝛ and dignity : and in ẙ
end, in theyꝛ countryes quarrell , conſecrated themſelues
as baliaunt and bowed beſſels , to gloꝛy and immoꝛtality.
Lucius Marcius, euen he , which in Spayne recouered ẙ
Romaine Empyꝛe , there foꝛe ſhꝛunken and fallen downe
to the ground,was boꝛne of ſimple and pooꝛe parentage,yet
thꝛough puiſſaunce obtayned in his countrey great honoꝛ
& a pꝛincipal dignity.What ſhould I recite Marcus Porci-
us Cato , a man much commended foꝛ his wiſedome and
pollicy?To what end ſhould I ſpeak of Marcus Marcellus
who firſt gaue Haniball the ouerthꝛow, & ſhewed playnly,
that the way to ouercome,was by pꝛowes and baliantnes.
Agayne why ſhoulde I omitt Marius that woꝛthye wight
and a thowſand moe being no gentlemen boꝛne,which not-
withſtanding.thꝛough theyꝛ paſſing ſkill and experience in
feates of Armes were aduaunced to honour,and pꝛomoted
to high eſtate,leauing to poſterity fame and immoꝛtalitye.
Herehence the armes and cognizaunces of honoꝛ and no-
bleneſſe,which euen in theſe our dayes are boꝛne , and had
right woꝛthely in eſtimation , did fetch their oꝛiginall
and firſt beginning . Foꝛ when any man had in battayle
ſhewed ſome notable poynt of a good baliaunt ſouldiar, he
was by the Generall made a gentleman, & had ſome badge
oꝛ token therof aſſigned vnto him,wherby his bloud might

be ennobled, through the prayse and glozye whereof his of=
spring might be in like maner prickeD with the deſire of
fame and commendation. Therefoze ſome haue in their
ſcochins, Caſtles engraué, geuing fozth therby the ſtrong
holdes, foztes, ſtraightes, ſcôces and paſſages, that were by
them in warre wonne and báquiſhed: other ſome, ringes oz
bendes, oz any other thing foz the number of enemies which
they had in ſome doubtfull and daungerous baitaile ſub=
dued. Other haue in theyz ſchochins ſtarres, ſigniſiyng per=
caſe that they bzought in ſome darcke and cloudy calamity,
no ſmall light and comfozt to the miſerable afflicted ſtate of
their natiue countrye, by this it is playne that foztitude
openeth the way to wozſhippe, and bzingeth vs moſt redy=
ly to the beholding the excæding bzight and cleare nature
of true nobility. *And to the end you may vndoubtedly diſcerne
the true value of a man, and know aſſuredly where fortitude is,
where puiſſaunce, where that high and lofty minde dwelleth: the
calamities which doe equally aſſault aſwell the noble as baſe=
borne, ſome with griefe, ſome with feare, ſome with terror, ſome
with trembling, may yelde vs a plaine and vndeceiueable marck
and teſtimony. For where puiſſaunce and fortitude is, there is
ingraffed a minde not to faynt for any trouble, not to diſpayre in
any perrill, not to languiſh in any woe and greeuous miſery, yea
if Fortune frowne, if daunger & death enſue, a worthy mind will
not be forgetfull. So that nothing may alike ſhew a gentle and
valiant hart, thē not to be vãquiſhed: which is ſeene in ſorrow,
tried in trouble, proued in perſecution.*

Gate. *Nothing might haue bene ſayd (in my ſimple opinion)
more truely and with better proofe. For euen as contented ſuffe=
raunce in the extremeſt and bittereſt cruelty, proueth the mind
to be high and diuine, as ſtedfaſtnes in a ſtate neuer ſo vnſtay=
ed & tottering, argueth an vncõquered value: So truely, time=
rouſnes in terror and daunger bewrayeth the faynt and feeble=
neſſe of a baſe and cowardly nature.*

Blandy. *No maruaile is it therefore if they which haue not*

bene dismayd at the terror of death, they which haue with most
valiaunt courage suffered bodely tormentes , they that would
for no manner of griefe be disturbed in minde, and do any thing
to stayne their honour and estimation, haue bene alwayes had in
great admiration. The prayse and glory whereof, springeth frō
the contempt of death.

Cate. Is the contempt of death in all men equally hono=
red? Dr may all those alike be wozthely commended, that
would willingly dye?

Blandy. You haue (I assure you) moued me a questiō right
profitable, and not vnfitt to be handled in this place . For
many, yea to to many there are , who being thzowne down
from an happy and pleasing state of life, do abide that hard=
nesse , & fœle in theyr flesh and natures such vnaccustomed
bitternesse, that they haue receiued into theyr hartes a vo=
luntary disposition to depart from life, and therefoze in an
extreme desperation of chaunge , and better foztune, doe
themselues to death : who notwithstanding are of many
thzough ignozaunce vndeseruedly commended , whereby
you may note, that the strength and fozce of true vertue is
such, that the counterfayte shewe thereof stirreth vp some,
both to admire and commēd a lott, rather lamentable, then
laudable. For I condemne them vtterly guilty of dastardly
cowardise , foz that they hasten theyr dying day, not at all
shewing thereby theyr constancy, but rather a minde van=
quished and subdued thzough a small tast of vading misery.
Other there are which offer themselues to daunger, not
with iudgemēt , and pzudent aduise, but being pzicked foz=
ward with a certayne rage oz fury of minde conceiued ei=
ther vnfayned, enuy, oz some other earnest & hoat affection.
Some other there are, y aduenture a daungerous attempt,
being moued thereunto with a very earnest hope , oz with
a desperate feare of their pzesent estate. Such, except they
had some certayne hope to escape daunger, oz gayne some
pziuate commodity , oz els were past all hope of escaping,

The Caftle of Pollicye.

would be neuer perſwaded to come to daunger) therefoze
ſith they miſſe the true & god purpoſe of Action, they may
alſo want the honour due vnto ſo great and noble a vertue.

Gate. What is the purpoſe oz marke whereunto this action, this contempt of death ſhould be directed, which alſo
winneth vs that high renowne and glozy?

Blandy. The marke and end which this contempt of death
ought to reſpect and loke vpon, is the glozy of Chziſt, the
honoz of our Pzince, the cauſe of our countrye, the defence
of our name and honeſty. They that venture theyz liues
foz theſe poyntes, are appoynted in the right courſe and
race of true honoz : foz that they obtayne the true and vndoubted end of vertue : wherefoze all other that purpoſe
vnto themſelues riches fame and glozy depending on
the conſent of the vnlettered multitude, and reſpect not the
true ſoueraygne god, they are rather to be accompted men
puft vpp with vayne deſire, and ambition, then valiant and
couragious men.

Gate. *You haue (me thinkes) not vnlearnedly diſcourſed of*
fortitude: wherein I cannot eaſelie comprehende, whether my
profitt or pleaſure hath bene greater, both which your penn yel-
deth to all thoſe that happelie peruſe your labours. It remay-
neth that you ſpeake of Temperance and Prudence, which
diſplayed, the maieſty of a King will appeare moze liuely
and apparant. Wherefoze ſay on I moſt hartely pzay you.

Blandy. Temperance ſtandeth in the true and iuſt mode-
ration of our actions, comming from a kinde of pzopentiõ,
oz inclynation, which is moſt dæpely by nature in vs im-
pzinted. And that you may moze plainely conceiue the pzoperty, and wozthyneſſe of this vertue, thus when we talke
of Temperance we vſe to diſpute. There is in vs a kinde
of power, inferioz to reaſon, yet her next handmayd, wherby we fæle in vs a pzones to be this oz that way affected.
The affection therefoze that is ingendzed by this faculty, is

ſuch

such, that as it is most fitt , good and necessary, so if it wat=
cheth not the direction, and as it were the finger poynt of
reason, it is intollerable. & bredeth oft our woe and confu=
sion. For by nature we ware hoate, angry, and cholericke,
naturally we loue, naturally we loth, we pitty, we despise,
we feare, we frowne, we desire, we disdayne, we are mar=
uailously by kinde stirred vp with ioy and pleasure. Which
affections before they become actions , least they should ex=
cede theyr iust due and proportion , and turne thereby to
our annoy, are to be tempered and moderated by reasons
rule and discipline. This man therefore that can thus go=
uerne, and moderate the motions of the minde, hath wonne
the loue of Temperaunce , and shall be honored of all men
as one indued with a rare , and singular vertue . The af=
fections therefore of the minde , as ire, loue, pleasure, and
the solace it selfe of lyfe, with many other are not (as igno=
raunt men suppose) to be raced out , but rather with the
light and flame of reason in the best and highest mindes
enkindled. Lyke as in the sea, such quiet & calme weather
is not to be desired , wherewith the floud may not be with
the least puffe of winde troubled, but rather such open aire
wherby the shipp at the stearne may sulck the Seas with
a mery gale and prosperous winde: euen so there is to be
desired in y minde a puffe , & as it were, a blowing billow
to hoyse vpp the sayles of the minde , whereby the course
thereof may be made more swift & certayne. And euen as
a skilfull & couragious horseman doth not alway delight
in a soft and gentle pace, but sometymes geueth his horse
the spurre , to the end his steede should moue more liuely:
So by reason, sometymes the affections of the minde are
styrred, and prycked forward, that we might more chere=
fully dispatch our busines. You know by these , what Te=
peraunce is, wherein it doth consist , and by what meanes
it is attayned.

Gate. My minde hitherto hath his content , striue and

fyzre at all to the contrary I may not, except you be silẽt:
wherefoze fay on, fo fhall you bzing me a fwæte reft.

Blandy. It foloweth that I fhew you my opiniõ of pzudẽce:
which vertue is the very ornamẽt and garland of the other
two , without which , they befoze fpoken of , can no
wife flozifh , and geue out kindely their cleare and bzight
lights of glozye, the want whereof , maymeth the minde
of a king. Pzudence therefoze refteth in the knowledge of
ciuile gouernement : which learneth vs not onely to go=
uerne wifely our felues, and families, but to rule poletik=
ly great Cittyes and Commonwealthes . And that you
may fully vnderftand , by what meanes this vertue is at=
tayned , it is right neceffary, ꝑ expediẽt you call to minde,
how men liuing as Barbarians , in woods and defolate
places were bzought to ozder, and at length perfwaded to
lyue vnder one lawe embzacing mutuall loue , ꝑ all kinde
of humanitye. Wherefoze, if the fwætenes and excellencie
of eloquence in antiquitie fo much pzeuailed , that men
were with ẏ mellodious harmonye thereof, dzawen from
barbaroufnes , to ciuilytye : If puiffance in the beginning
repelled iniuries , and became thereby the rœte of roy=
altye : if gœd and pzofitable lawes ftayed moft faftly, men
thus reclaymed and bzought to the quiet and happy home
of peace and reft: I holde the onely redye and perfect ftepp
to trace out pzudence, by the loue of Eloquence, by the ho=
noz of chiualrye, by the knowledge and ftudye of the ciuile
lawes . Foz thefe fciences are right wozthely reckoned a=
mong thofe which are the moft chiefe ꝑ higheft : foz ẏ they
haue bene the founders of Citties , the fafegard of com=
mon focietye , the pzincipall ftay and rocke of all noble and
flozifhing Commonwealthes . *To be prudent in a priuate*
man , is right worthely commended: in a king , in a prince , and
in the place of Maieftye it geueth out fuch comfortable bea-
mes , that thoufands and infinite numbers thereby, receaue re-
liefe : For her propertye is, to be diligent, and bufie for the weale
of

of all. They are therefoze in no wise to be deemed pzudent, which seeke the aduauncement of themselues, and the preferment of any one pziuate Familye. Wherefoze, if you to your expectation, and our wished and laboured intent, purpose to behold the high and hautye hue of the Maiestye of a king, marke and impzint deeply in your minde, what bziefly insueth. A king therefoze, as it appeareth by the discourse pzecedent, came of no small beginning, deriued, and spzinging of no other roote, then an honozable and royall hart, garnisht, and deckt with all worthye, and noble vertues *So that this king which we speake of, and haue through the viewe, and consent of many famous and worthy writers, chosen to be chiefe in this our Comwonwealth, is such a one, whose Scepter iustice raysed, whose soueraigntye fortitude defendeth, whose preheminence prudence ruleth, whose prerogatiue temperaunce keepeth in most safe and quiet estate.* Which chiefe and pzincipall vertues, reste alwayes in perpetuall mouing, the motion whereof bzingeth fozth aboundantly bzaunches oz rather (if you please) buddes, which cann be by no irkesome and sharpe aire blasted, foz that the sapp and iuice of this tree in euery bzaunch and twigge thereof continually equally flozisheth, being subiect to no tyme and season. *Herehence mercy floweth, herehence mildenes, herehence courtesie, affabilitye, liberalitye, prouidence, loue, which maruelously graceth the maiestye of a king.* This is also to be required & chiefely looked foz, of a King, ý what noble acte soeuer he take in had, whether it appertayne to ciuile gouernmet in tyme of peace, oz to martiall pzowes, in tyme of warre, his clearenes and excellencye, geue most manifest notice and signification, that he setteth no stoze by humaine thinges, but doth with most earnest indeuour & intention of minde, affect those thinges that be heauenly, and euerlasting. This high and lofty intention of minde causeth the Peeres and nobilitye of his nation, with all dutye and reuerence to behold him, styrreth all good men with

The Castle of pollycye.

all loue and honoz to embzace him , fozceth all bafe and vile minded men to feare and tremble at his fight and pze= fence.

Gatc. As you in our Warch difcourfed in this manner, and came to the lyke iſſue, you haue hitherto bent the dzift of your vnderſtanding, I with many moe (if you remem= ber well) caufed you to cutt of the reſt (fpeaking to our fimple opinions fufficiently) you would haue fayd , of the Waieſtye of a king. *Minding you of a Queene by diſtance of place then farre of, yet by nature neare, by due comparſon of whoſe excellēt cleare brightnes, either that haue bene in any monument of Antiquitye honorably ſpoken of, or liue at this preſent Chriſtened in magnificence, merited moſt high renoume: that when her excellencye was named, all our powers and ſpi= rites were in a manner ſurpriſed with ioy and pleaſure, behol= ding through your ſpeach as in a glaſſe, her great guiſtes, rare vertues, and noble gouernement. At what tyme all wee (moſt lowly proſtrating our ſelues) with one voyce aſſēted, that Q. Eli= zabeth our moſt high & noble maiſtres, ſhould ſuffice, not onely vs her true, fayth full, & naturall ſubieſts; but all other peeres, of what kinde of people they ſprang of, of what noble lyne & paren= tage they deſcended, to behold in her excellencie, the true and abſolute Maieſtye of a Prince and gouernour : wiſhing then moſt earneſtly, that one among vs had a penn of that propertie, that either he could at once write all lāguages, or that all natiōs could vnderſtand what he wrote. Then not onely Europe which at this preſent ringes of her glory, but all the world beſides, ſhould haue knowledge and vnderſtanding of his ſouerainge La= dy and Maiſtres.*

Blandy. I can not eaſely forgett, what ioy and pleaſure we tooke of that honorable report, wherein as we then reſted in the cogi= tation of ſo rare and royall an example. ſo I thinke it fitt to fi= niſhe our ſpeach of this firſt and chiefe piller of our Common= wealth: directing all other that would vnderſtād more through= ly, of the perfection of a Prince (which nothing ſheweth forth
more

more liuely then example) to the beholding our most gracious
Queene and gouernour:whose fayth in Christian Religiõ,whose
knowledge in learning,whose pollicie in gouerning,whose clemē-
cy in pardoning,whose bountifulnesse in preferring,whose pitti-
full and tender commiseration of the poorest wretch that liueth
within her dominiõs,doth not without great cause establish her
louing subiects in honoring her,powring out dayly most feruent-
ly their prayers for her safe , long,and prosperous gouernement.
God of his infinite mercy and goodnesse keepe her to raigne long
ouer vs.

Gate. It seemeth now therefoꝛe right good, you speake of
the Iusticer.

Blandy. I will most gladly doe my indeuour. The two
limmes that chiefly and aboue other, strengthē the body of
Princely maiestie, is the Iusticer and souldiar. The charge of
which is great and honoꝛ acquired thereby right woꝛthely
had in estimation:The one executeth the will of his *Soue-*
raigne vpon the offender at home, and in the Citty, the o-
ther wꝛeaketh the indignation of the Prince in the field,vp-
on the body of his enemy. The one is chosen foꝛ his pꝛudence, the other foꝛ his pꝛudence, and puissaunce, the one
foꝛ his rightfull dealing, the other foꝛ his vpꝛight minde,
exposing his body to all perrils,to all pouerty,to all lacke.
The one with his toung kæpeth peace, the other with the
swoꝛd restoꝛeth peace in daunger,& clean lost to his foꝛmer
state. So that whereas both shoot at one pꝛincipall marcke
(foꝛ the good and perfect souldiar hath two marckes and
endes of his action, the one victoꝛy, wherein he winneth
honoꝛ,moꝛe pꝛiuate:the other peace, wherby he returneth
triumphantly to receiue of his Pꝛince and countrey the titles due to so great desart,which maketh his foꝛmer honoꝛ
which I befoꝛe named moꝛe pꝛiuate, moꝛe publicke, moꝛe
knowē, moꝛe ample and gloꝛious)yet sith the meanes differ not a litle,wherby the iusticer is pꝛomoted to his degræ,and the souldiar aduaunced to an honoꝛable calling in

                                                    the

the commonwealth I cannot finde in my poore and simple consideration, but that the souldiar in his proper right
may challenge a kinde of superiozity of the Lawyer.

Gate. I cannot gaynesay your position, which is that the
souldiar and iusticer prefire befoze theyz mindes one end
and purpose, so that I am induced to thinke clearely, that
whereas the meanes are differing, oddes to be therefoze
betwixt theyz both desertes. Foz what can the iusticer haz-
sard in peace, where the enemy is repelled, where foƶce is
subdued, where fury is put to flight ? his treasure, wealth,
wife and childƶen, are by the lawes, as with a sure and
strong foƶte)defended his name and honesty, a number of
lately richt clients (with earnest and difficult suites subdued) garde, his health phisicke pzeserueth . On the other
side the souldiar so litle estemeth safety at home, content in
his mate, pleasure in his childzen, solace with his friendes,
that where his fidelity to his *Prince* , loue to his countrey,
honoz of his vpzight minde, shall be bƶought in question,
and stand to be tryed, he will not onely most willingly foƶ-
goe all these, but cherefully bow and consecrate his lusty
limmes to tiresome labours, his body richly clad, to pin-
ching nakednesse, his feeding nature, to staruing hunger,
his fresh and liuely lookes to lothsome languishing : his si-
nowes to be seuered, his ioyntes to be cut in two, his bloud
to be spilt, his carcase to be stamp to dyzt & myƶe. Wherefoze I see no reason but that the souldiar may in the common wealth be pzeferred befoze the iusticer.

Blandy. Albeit it be a matter very difficult to iudge, whether
should be pzeferred befoze other, sith the vertue in a iusticer and souldiar are not of one kinde (although they pzicke
at one marcke) and that it farre passeth the reach of either
of our capacityes to waygh their pziuate vertues so differing, in equall ballances, leauing therefoze the controuer-
sie to be decided by men of deeper iudgement, and ryper
experience, notwithstanding I thinke it most fitt the iusticer

cer not vnworthply(if his calling and condition of life be
well examined) to haue the second place in this our commonwealth. For where you reason thus, that the souldiar
doth hassard more then the iusticer, fearing no force, drea-
ding no daunger, prising no perrill whereby his honoura-
ble minde should be more seene and appear (with lofty and
high courage I cannot with words sufficiently commend)
yet your reasō is infæbled by this, that it is agaynst the nature of peace, and therefore much agaynst the duety, order
and course of good magistrates, to suffer (as much as in thē
lyeth)any such iniurious action to be committed, whereby
the stomake of the least man should be so tried and proued.
The actions are not of one kinde, for that they take not the
like beginning, although they haue the like end and direction. Agayne a reason springing of one singuler Action, to
conclude in generality, a better or worse hath small, or rather no force at all. Wherefore sithe you made mention of
fortitude and magnanimity as though the souldiar onely,
and not the iusticer did regarde and embrace so greate and
noble a vertue, and might be condemned of dastardly cowardise, I haue thought it good and expedient to cleare so
high and estimable a calling, of so base & foule a crime. First
therefore, whereas it is most manifest that the minde of
the iusticer and souldiar is occupyed about one thing, that
is, peace and tranquility, the one to keepe it alwayes florishing, the other to restore it decaying and in daunger, here
it would be demaunded, whither the honour of the iusticer
is not as great and nobler in preseruing common quiet, or
the worthinesse of the souldiar to be more extolled in pur-
chasing & redæming peace pressed and throwen downe to
the ground. Wherefore (that this doubt and controuersy
may more clearely appeare) shew (I hartely pray you)
wherein honor resteth and by what meanes it is atchiued.
Gate. Honor depēdeth of the iust measure of value showē
in the defence of a good cause.

E.iiij.

Blādy.

Blandy. How then may value be knowen?

Gate. Value springeth of contention, contention of two mindes contraryly affected. So that where there is an assault, and defence, the defender is to winne honor by hys value, which perswadeth him during life to vpholde and maintaine the right of the cause.

Blandy. If so, the value of the iusticer will anone more eminently and clearely shine then the vertue of the souldiar. *Who doth not holde it a harder matter to kill a secret, then an open enemy?* The iusticer and souldiar carry and vpholde both an honorable minde. The souldiar standes readely furnisht to fight in the fielde, where he may looke round about: The iusticer is inclosed in a little cell or studdy, where he may be secretly slayne. The souldiar hath warning y the enemy approacheth by the neighing of barbd horses, ratling of men of armes, sound of trumpet, Phife and drumme: The iusticer hath foreknowledge also, but by a more sely and feeble noyse, as a dores creeke, knacke, and whisper. The souldiar seeth men glittering as white as siluer: The iusticer seeth one man offering enbost workemanshipp like fire and Angels of golde. The souldiar fighteth commonly man to man. The iusticer is inuaded sometimes at once with no lesse then twenty men. And wheras the iusticer and souldiar (sith we all professe Christ) directe their Actions to eternity, to euerlastingnesse, to that blessed and endlesse felicity, and that the iusticer is assaulted although after an other manner, as egerly of his enemy in the chamber, as the souldiar prouoked to fight in the fielde with his deadly foe (I speake not here of a bodely death, but of a death whereunto bodye and soule through offence is subiect) and that peace is to be preferred before warres, for which we dayly pray, the officers and magistrates in peace, and therefore the iusticer their chiefe and principall, shall haue the second place in this commonwealth: as one that will not harken to corruption, much lesse suffer his minde to be abused and defiled

with

loith bʒibery. Foʒ woe, woe, may that cōmonwealth crie,
if they which ſitt in iudgement will be by any maner of en-
tiſementes allured and wonne from the ſwæte and ſacred
countenaunce of iuſtice. In conſideration whereof, this
realme of England is in my opinion in this poynt thʒiſe
happy and bleſſed.

Gate. Uerely I thinke no leſſe, if the Lawyers of this
Realme foʒ the moſt part with theyʒ companies, did as
well imitate the vertue and ſincere dealing, as they daylye
beholde the grauity of the iudges of this land: their oʒder
ſhould not at this pʒeſent be ſubiect to a deſerued diſgrace:
ſuch rebuke, ſuch repʒoch, ſhould not follow thoſe fellow-
ſhippes, and houſes of courte, where gentlemen deſcended
of noble Parentage, liue, and ſuppoſe themſelues to trace
the ſteppes of honoʒ and woʒſhipp.

Blandy. What ſay you?

Gate. I ſpeake not againſt the law, foʒ without it no
kingdome can ſtand. The good and well minded Lawyer I
greatly reuerence. The young Gentlemen which come
thither either to ſtudy the law, oʒ to appʒoue what exerciſe
and condition of life may beſt ſitt theyʒ noble natures, I
highly commend: wiſhing my ſelfe as able to perſwade thē
the beſt, as they are of a good inclination tractable. The ré-
nant which retayne no good thing, I would (with all lowly
duety and ſubmiſſion to the ſtate I ſpeake it) were well
imployed.

Blandy. Are any of this pʒofeſſion idle and vnoccupyed.

Gate. It were better they were idle, then ſo ocupied.

Blandy. Is it poſſible?

Gate. This is the blowing billow, you in your bodye pʒo-
poʒtioned ſpake of befoʒe, which defoʒmeth all other parts.
This is ẏ moʒtiferous & deadly woʒme, which hath almoſt
with his eger and perpetuall gnawing and biting, woʒne
the legges to the bone. This is the impoſtumation, which
if it be not in time pʒicked, will with his ſtincking contagiō

poyſon

poifon all. This ozder is the nurfe & mother of thofe mates, which at their feafons ftyzre hither and thither to moue bzawles. It is a wozlde to beholde, what new and ftraunge natures they haue clapt on, how they transfozme them felues. There, where there is no hope of gayne, he ftådeth as he thinketh gaylye, but yet (as he is) a counterfaite, loking to be wozfhipped, and will not ftick (fo bnmanerly a puppye he is) to take the bpper place of right good gentle= men. Here, the fame man hoping to gayne of a pooze and fimple clowne of the Countrye foztye pence, is become his flaue and dzudge. *O that Georgias Leontinus did lyue in fome Englifh mans hart and ftomack: who reprouing the rulers of Lariffa becaufe they had receaued into the company of plea- ders any kinde of people, was wont to fay : that euen as plafte- rers of any kynde of ftuffe, would make Morter, or any thing of lyke fort: So there were fo conning craftifmê in Lariffa, which of any condition and kinde of men would make a Lawyar.* Cice- ro the moft famous ozatoz and learned in the lawes that euer Rome nourifht (whê they bzake their lifts and lymits & grewe difozdered) nippeth moft wifely thofe of his owne ozder, in this mäner. Proueniüt nobis oratores noui, ftul- ti adolefcêtuli. So that I pzay God moft hartely, it fareth not with bs the inhabitants of this noble Iland, as it did after the fozewarnings and fhewes of thefe two (not fo faythfull to their Countrye, as infœne in the ftate of their Commonwealth) with the people of Lariffa and the Cit= tizens of Rome. Foz not long after, thefe people and flozi= fhing Citties, fell downe headlong to the ground. Foz how was it poffible, that the ftate of thofe Empires could long ftand ftedfaft, when the chiefe and pzincipall pillers that fhould fuffeyne the waight and burthen of fo huge, fo high, fo honozable and ample a gouernement, became rot= ten. Which ruine and ouerthzowe of the whole Common= wealth appeared then, not fo much by decayed houfes which were aunciêt & of great nobility, as by erecting mä=

nozs

noꝛs where Dyꝛt and Dong was found . *In conſideration
whereof, I let to ſpeake of the hills and mountaynes rayſed, lands
and poſſeſſions purchaſed, aboundance of wealth gathered and
forſt together by men in our nation, neither wiſe, nor learned,
politike, nor prudent, temperate, liberall, nor pitifull .*

Blandy. Is it not a poynt and chiefe poynt (thinke you) of
great pollicye and wiſedome , to aduaunce our ſtock and
family? Is it not in the opinion of moſt men a happy thing
to be rich ? Doe not all men Delight in , and therefoꝛe Deſire
a fayꝛe, large and beautifull houſe? To be Loꝛd of many
Mannoꝛs, to receaue many reuenewes , Doth it not in=
gender great fauour, bring much woꝛſhipp and reuerence?
Gate. If you folowe herein the iudgement of the multi=
tude I aſſent . If you foꝛgett their blinde and groſſe Imagi=
nations, and cleaue to the aſſured and vndeceaueable direc=
tions of wiſe men, you ſhall bꝛiefely vnderſtand , what is
ſæmely in, and beſt becommeth a Lawyar . Where the
the minde is ſtyꝛred with a deſier to be aduaunced , and to
rayſe his name and bloud , frō a meane to a higher Degræ,
there is the minde ſo vered with Diuerſitye , that at length
it yeldeth to ſome great and greuous extremitye. But whē
the minde is taught , that the chiefe and ſoueraigne good
reſteth in an honeſt and vertuous lyfe , there are the cogi=
tations calme and ſwæte , there content holdeth deſier re=
ſtrayned from any ambitious affection. This man that is
thus affected , ſæketh altogether to pleaſe and inrich his
minde, pꝛouideth foꝛ no moꝛe then will ſuffiſe nature, hol=
Deth it a perilous thing to be rich, and is aſſuredly perſwa=
Ded, that aboundance and flowing of woꝛldly wealth , ra=
ther hindereth then helpeth , rather plucketh Downe then
erecteth the courage and aſpiring minde of a noble na=
ture. The Iuſticer therefoꝛe and Lawiar which is the right
hand of a Pꝛince ought (if he purpoſe to kæpe the ſtate ꝼ
condition of his lyfe cleare and vnſteyned) to lyue in the
contemplatiō of inſtice , fæde and nouriſh his minde with
                    F. ij.   the

the loue of bertue : thinking it a thing farr vnfitt for his
high calling to be dæmed in his deſiers a Marchaunt, in
his order and courſe of lyfe, an artificer. The Souldiar,
who hath the third place in this Cōmonwealth (of whoſe
lyfe, nature, and properye we purpoſe preſently to treate
of) yeldeth the deſire of riches to the Marchaunt: dæming
it for his condition of lyfe and profeſſion, a foule matter to
be addicted to ſuch traſh, dyrt, and pelfe.

Blandy. Syr, you haue ſpoken ſo truely of the lyfe and
condition of a Lawyer, that I thinke the good and better
part of the profeſſors of the law, will yelde you, (not without your deſart) a good opinion, ſo farre is it vnlikely, that
any other will cōceaue offēce. I ſtand now attētiue to heare
your diſcourſe of a Souldiar, in which kinde of lyfe, you,
euen from your græne and tender yeares, haue bene trayned, and therefore may learne me the more readily, what
is in him moſt decent and chiefly required.

Gate. In this caſe I thinke it moſt expedient and neceſſa-
rye, I ſort a Souldiar firſt into his diuerſitye, or rather
braunches, which knowen, you ſhall more playnely vnderſtand what he is. All theſe therefore are conteyned
within the name of a Souldiar. The Generall, high Martiall with his Prouoſtes, Serieant generall, Serieant of a
regiment, Corownell, Captayne, Liuetenent, Auncient,
Serieant of a Company, Corporall, gentleman in a company or of the Rounde, Launce paſſado: theſe are ſpeciall, the other that remaine, priuate or commō Souldiars.
The Profeſſion as well of the cōmon, as priuate Souldiar is honorable, which reſteth in the maintenaunce to
death, of a good and rightfull cauſe: the condition no leſſe
paynefull then full of perill, the qualify, cleane, diligent,
duetifull, delighting rather in braue furniture and glittering armor, then in deynty dyet, womanlyke wantonnes,
and bayne pleaſures. It is fitt he be not onely ſkilfull in
the weapon he bſeth, but alſo in any other that his ſtrength
                                                    will

will geue him to handle and winne at his pleasure and cō-
maundement. It is also to be required he hath the skill and
qualitye of Swimming, lykewise in Marching, turning,
retyzing, sighting to obserue the ozder by his Captayne
pzescribed: Such a one may be called a good trayned souldiar, and if he be ignozaunt hereof, although he hath bene
twentye yeares in ẏ warres, I accompte him not wozthy
the name of a Souldiar. Finally the onely & chiefe grace,
that beautifieth the minde of a Souldiar, is the cōtempt of
Spoyle, and refusall of riches. Foz the cozrupt opinion
of wealth and pleasures, are the enemies of verue, the al-
lurements not to so fond, as wicked endeuozs.

Blandy. You haue not vnskilfully deliuered your opinion of a Souldiar in generall. Now, if you would bziefely
set downe the duety that belongeth to euery seuerall officer, you should highly pleasure me. what is therefoze to
be desired in a Generall of an Armye?

Gate. A Generall ought first and chiefely behold the Maiestye of God, and cause therefoze his true Religion in his
Armye to be had in due reuerence: in such sozt, that his
Souldiars may perceaue he is in dœde Religious. And lett
him by all meanes cause the Pziestes and Ministers of
his holy will and testament, in his Armye to retayne
their dignitye, and to be esteemed and reuerenced of his
Souldiars. Foz if the very Paynims by due obseruations
of their fayned Religion, did kœpe their Armies in marue-
lous obedience and ozder: how much moze shall true Religion, deliuered from our Lozd and Sauiour, pzeuaile a
Generall, and Armye that loueth him, to the atchieuing
great and miraculous victozyes. Also the Generall ought
to be modest, pzudent, and temperate, geuen to no ryot
and excesse, neither miserably bent to filthy lucre. It stā-
deth greatly on him to auoyd the name of a vaunter: which
is sœne in this, that he doe not vendicate to himselfe alone
the pzayse of good successe: but do impute the same first to

God. Secondly to his Captaynes. Thirdly to his Souldiars. Furthermoꝛe it behoueth a Generall to be a noble
Gentleman, trayned vp in thoſe ſciences, thꝛough the
knowledge whereof, he ſhall ſooner attayne that perfection, which in a Generall is nædefull. Laſtly, foꝛ that I
ſtudy herein bꝛeuitye, moued thereunto, thꝛough great
and wayghty occaſions, a Generall muſt be religious, temperate, ſober, wiſe, valiant, liberall, curteous, Eloquent, ꝭ
of good fame and reputation.

Blandy. What haue you to ſay of the hygh Martiall.

Gate. The duety of the high martiall is as great in a
Campe, as the office of a iuſticer in peaceable and ciuile gouernement. To him appertayneth the true adminiſtration
of iuſtice, the hearing and determining of controuerſies, ꝭ
the puniſhing of diſoꝛders. And therefoꝛe as he ought of
of himſelfe to be a man, both graue, wiſe, learned, and tho-
rowly well experienced in martiall affayꝛes: ſo is it alſo
conuenient foꝛ him to haue about him men of iudgement,
ſkilfull in military diſcipline, and lawes of a Campe, redi-
ly to reſolue of euery queſtion, accoꝛding to equity and iuſtice. This belōgeth next ꝭ imediately (as part of his pꝛincipal charge) to ẏ high martiall, that he receiue the names
and numbers of all the Corownets of hoꝛſe, and companies of footemen that are in the Armye: he muſt alſo lear-
nedly pꝛopoꝛtion and caſt, what ſcope of ground will ſuffice
to encampe them with all theyꝛ pꝛouiſion, Carriadges, ꝭ
Munition. The high Martiall muſt aſſigne euery battaile
his conuoy, and guide, oꝛ two, to bꝛing them moſt eaſye
wayes.

Blandy. Pꝛocæd (I pꝛay you) to the Serieaunt Generall,
oꝛ Maioꝛ, ꝭ Serieaunt of a Regiment.

Gate. This Officer ought to be a man of great courage
and well experienced, that he be not diſmayd with the terroꝛ of the enemies pꝛeſence. Foꝛ the moſt part of all hys
actiōs are to be exployted euen in the face of the enemy: he
ought

ought to be a man therefore of liuely spirite, and quicke inuention, that he may soddenly perceiue, and quickely conceiue the nature of the Scituation, and order of the Enemies aray, altering and disposing accordingly of his owne. His duty is to attend the Lord high martiall, or Lieutenant Generall to receiue direction in what sort they pleasure is, the Army that day shall march, he ought to haue a rolle of all the bandes, and in euery band, what number of short weapons, what Pikes, and what shot, and the same to haue alway about him: that if any want, he may admonish the Muster Mayster and Treasurer thereof, to the end there be according to the want, a fit and conuenient supply. To this Officer it appertayneth so to ranck his souldiars, that the best armed inpale the rest, and that the force and flankes of his battayles be armed with pikes, the Ensignes well garded with halberdes, the tayle well enclosed with y Cariages, winges of shot on eyther side, and those winges more or lesse, accordingly as the place is larger and straighter, stroger or weaker, on the one or on y other side. Those winges represent the flankers in fortification and ought as orderly to flancke and skoure before the face of the battayle as bulwarkes do the Curtayne of a Towne or fort.

Blandy. Procede now I pray you to the office and duty of a Corownell.

Gate. It appertayneth chiefly to a Corownell after the Prince hath elected him, to make a good and singuler choise of his Captaynes and Officers, that they may the better and more readely take good order for the good execution of any seruice. It is most requisite he hath nere vnto his perso certayne wise, expert, and valiant Gentlemen, that be able both quickely to conceiue, and plainely and sensibly to vtter the cause of any new accident, or thing whatsoeuer, that he shall see. It behoueth him to take great heed, least the souldiars in his Regiment be discouraged for want of necessary prouission, but in such sort be prouided for, that the soul-

ars may grow into a liking of their Captaynes. It ſhalbe
an honozable part in a Corownell ſometime to lend of his
owne to his Captaynes, that they may in like maner ayde,
and binde therefoze their ſouldiars to them in theyz wants
and extremitye. And aboue all other thinges, let a Corownell take héed that he be not noted to be a piller of the ſouldiars , oz to play the Marchaunt making his gayne bpon
them: and as it behoueth him to cleare himſelfe alwayes
by the contrary action, of ſo foule & diſhonozable a crime, ſo
it ſtandes him greatly on, that his Captaynes be not infected with the like cozruption. Foz there is nothing ſo repug-
nant to the honozable pzofeſſion of a Souldiar in generall,
and therefoze much moze of a Captayne, greater of a Coronell, as to be noted miſerable.

Blandy. What you haue ſayd, no man with reaſon oz knowledge can withſtand: I deſire now to be inſtructed of the duty of a Captayne, and his Lieutenaunt.

Gate. This déepe and pzincipall conſideration ought to
be in a Captayne , that a charge of the liues of men is to
him committed, ſo that if any quayle bnder his conduct, either by raſhnes oz by want of knowledge , he is to render
accompt thereof befoze ỹ great Judge . He ought not to be
couetous oz niggardly, neuer to kéepe backe his ſouldiars
pay, but by all meanes poſſible to pzocure them theyz pay,
and to his hability rewarding them ouer and aboue : foz by
that meanes he gayneth honoz, and lincketh them faſt and
aſſured to him in any doubtful & perilous ſeruice. A Lieue-
tenant alſo is an office of credit and reputation : but in the
abſence of his Captaine farr greater and déeper. In all fac-
tions oz queſtions among the Souldiars, it behoueth him
to be newtre , wozking moſt louingly pacification . It appertayneth to him to ouerſee the Serieantes and Corpo-
ralls , that they doe theyz duetye, and oftentimes to ayde
them with his owne perſon . He is to bſe moſt frendly and
bzotherly his Auncient, he ſhould be a man able to ſpeake
well

well and ſenſibly, and ſtudy by courteſy rather thẽ by ſeue⸗
ritye to frame aright, crooked and peruerſe mindes. It be⸗
honeth the Liuetenant, much moꝛe therefoꝛe the Captaine
to be continually Armed, as well when no perill is feared,
as in tyme of daunger, to geue example to the reſt of the
Souldiars, that they may not thinke their Armoꝛ bur⸗
thenous, but by vſe to make it as familiar to them, as their
clothes, ſhyꝛt, and ſkinne.

Blandy. If you will in lyke manner declare, what belon⸗
geth to an Auncient, Sericant of a company, and Corporall, you ſhall finiſhe a good and pꝛofitable laboꝛ.

Gate. The Auncient. and Enſigne bearer, ought to be a
man of good accompt, honeſt, and vertuous, that the Captayne may repoſe the rather moꝛe credite and affiance in
him: he ought to behaue himſelfe wiſely, diſcretely, and
ſoberly, that he be therefoꝛe moꝛe loued of the Souldiars:
conſidering thereby, ẏ not onely his owne perſon ſhall be
in moꝛe ſafetye, when he attempteth perilous exploytes,
but alſo the whole ſeruice moꝛe bꝛauely and honoꝛably ex⸗
ployted: foꝛ the value and vertue of the Auncient ſetteth
foꝛth the vertue, and valour of the Caprayne and whole
Company. The Sericaunt of a Company ought to be a
man choſen of quick ſpirite and actiue bodye: to the end he
be not ſtaggering and aſtonyed vpon new accidents, but
pꝛompt and readye on a ſoddayne, to doe that to him ap⸗
pertayneth. His duetye reſteth greatly, in oꝛdering and
rancking his Company, aſſigning to each Souldiar his
due place, cutting of bꝛaules, and all manner of conten⸗
tion. The Corporall is a degrée aboue the pꝛiuate Sould⸗
iar, and therefoꝛe he ſhould paſſe and ſurmount his inferi⸗
ours in witt, diſcretion, and diligence. The Corporall
ought to kéepe continuall company with his little troupe,
committed to his charge, to lodge with them, and pꝛouide
foꝛ their want, and to inſtruct them how to handle and vſe
the weapon they carry. He ought to remember perfectly,

how euery one is armed,and furnished, when he receaued them in charge, and to sée that no part therof be spoyled, but be preserued neate and trymme. Finally, the nature and qualitye of all good Souldiars is this, that they stand alwayes of their credite and reputation, accompting no losse of goods coparable, to a dishonourable foyle, to haue a great, high, and waightye respect of his charge, and to be no lesse carefull and zealous thereof, then euery honest and honorable gentleman, should take of his wife, familye, and children: In conclusion, to feare nothing so much (appeared it neuer so terrible to flesshe and bloud) as infamy. Thus you haue heard my poore conceit & opiniō, of a souldiar: also the duetyes of those, who haue a superioritye in that profession: deliuered I confesse, not so amply and in so comely manner, as the waightynes of the Argument would requier: but as the slendernes of my skill, would permitt me in this discourse to followe.

Blandy. Your treaty hitherto may counteruaile well, both your prowes, and profession. And whereas some other, grounded more in knowledge, could geue out a larger, and dæper drift, wheeunto you percase (if you were not shortly to be imployed otherwise) would to your power bend y reach of your capacitye: yet these briefe speaches may happely please, where heaped labors are found tyresome and vnseasonable. Wherefore, conuert your penne I hartely pray you, to the displaying the braue and worthye actions done by our nation in Friseland. Which performed, you shall discharge and accomplishe our both desiers.

Gate. Corownell Norris and his companyes, to y number of xi. Ensignes of footemen, and one Cornet of horsemen ariued in West Friseland, at a towne called Counder the xi. of July, where he was ioyfully receaued by the Graue van Hollock, by whose commaundement and aucthoritye the Souldiars were Forraied on the Boares for their refreshing, for the space of two dayes. Wherehence
being

being ſodenly called, we marched by night, and pitched in a place called Fornecloyſter neare to ȳ towne of Colleine : wherein were thȝœ Enſignes of Malecontentes, foȝ the defence of that place, well and ſtrongly foȝtified.

Blandy. Befoȝe you enter farther into this matter, J pȝay you ſhewe me what are theſe Malecontentes, that trouble ſo much thoſe Countries ?

Gate. Jt is a people that feareth neither God, noȝ man, cruell, bloudy, and beggarly, gathered together of the froth and ſcomme of many nations : Jn manners barbarous, in opinion Turquiſhe, hoping with a whott and earneſt indeuoȝ to ſpoyle and ſpill all Chȝiſtian bloud.

Blandy. Js it poſſible we ſhould haue ſuch helhoundes ſo neare bs ? Herein the mercye and louing kindenes of our heauenly Loȝd and Sauiour towardes bs, is to be magnified, and ſufferaunce towardes ſo curſed and peruerſe a generation to be maruailed at. Pȝocœde J pȝay you, in your taken in hand laboȝ.

Gate. Theſe Malecontents, whereof J made mention befoȝe, being at the receipte of their pay, when aduertiſement was bȝought them, that the Engliſhe men were in Fornecloyſter, were ſtricken with ſuch a feare, that omitting their pay, tœke their flight as it is wȝitten, no man folowing them. Unto which Cloyſter our Engliſhmen ariued. The day folowing our people remoued, marching to Vpſlaught where fiue Enſignes of the enemy were ſtrongly incoucht, furniſhed with Munition and 3. ſmall pœces of Artillarye, ſeuered in two places. The Graue van Hollock ſent a dȝúme to moue them to yeld bp thoſe foȝtes, without condition (ſauing their liues) to the bſe of the Pȝince of Dȝinge, ȥ the States, which they btterly refuſed to doe affirming their tenure to be plãſed in ȳ right of ȳ Popes holynes, ȥ the Countie De Lalyne. Whereunto the Graue replyed, that he would commend them ouer to the power and will of the Engliſhe Corownell. Whereupon

The Caſtle of pollycye.

vpon, the Coronell did beſett the places with his people ſo ſtraightly, that there was no way left fo₂ the enemy to eſcape. The Malecontents perceiuing themſelues ſo w₂apt and inuironed, by ſuch as they feared would haue no compaſſion, ſent fo₂th a D₂omme to craue mercye. The Engliſhe men were then ſo ſharpe ſett to deſtroy ſo helliſh a b₂ode. Notwithſtanding, whoſe heate and rage Coronell Norris committed the cauſe to the wi!l and pleaſure of the Graue, he permitted them to depart, their liues ſaued without Armes.

Blandy. Herein the ſteyed and reſolute wiſedome of Maiſter Norris deſerueth as equally to be p₂ayſed, as mercy in the Graue, as Pardon in ſo god and hono₂able a perſon.

Gate. On the next day in the mo₂ning our people diſlodged, marching towardes Grounning, the chiefe and p₂incipall Cittye in Friſeland poſſeſſed of the Enemye: within th₂e Engliſhe miles whereof, we were diſperſed into diuers villages thereaboutes, and ſo remained till the ſixt day of Auguſt. About xi. of the clocke of the ſame day, the Enempe gaue vs a Larum: In this caſe, leaſt that the enemy might thinke their Larū to haue any maner wayes touched vs with a ſhiuer of feare, but rather with a flame of furye, Coronell Morgaine, an expert and olde Souldiar, a noble & valiant Captayne, accompaned with Captayne Saliſbury, Captayne Chatterton, Captaine Corne, Liuetennant Carie, and Liuetenant Forder: with other Gentlemen and Souldiars of p₂ofe, to the number of 200 & mo₂e, went to diſcouer what that Larum was, w̄ a purpoſe ỹ if ỹ Enemy were a thow̄ſand, ſo that they were on fote, they ſhould know & fele p̄fo₂ce of Engliſhe blond.

Blandy. Behold here true value comming from a courage, moſt ſtedfaſtly ſetled in reſolute mindes.

Gate. In concluſiõ we happened on their maine battayle: At what tyme Captayne Corne, a man alwaye little d₂eading the Enemies p₂eſence, cried with a lowd voyce:

My

My Maiſters , and fellow Souldiars, my naturall and deare Countrymen ,let vs now ſtand faſt , and geue yonder curſed company a Canuaſſado, for the honor of our Prince and Countrye . Let them vnderſtand by our ſtomaches, what minde and ſpirite remaineth in the reſt , and by that which is found in the reſt, to be loked for of all our nation . This little ſayd , a charge was geuen.

Blandy. Who can with wordes ſufficiently commend the courage of this Captayne , the loftines of his high and honorable minde? This Corne was not great of bodye , a very graine in compariſon , yet yelding abundance of fine and white flower . This Corne ſmelled of no cockle, for that it grew, in ſo fertile, and ſappie a ſoyle. Let all ſouldiars therefore, that will fæde their mindes with the bread, which ſo noble Corne hath made , moulded and baken for them to eate, receaue him moſt worthely : in prayſe to preferre , in fidelitye to folow , in lyfe to imitate, in courage to commend , in prowes and true bertue deſeruedly to loue, honor , and reuerence . Now I pray you ſay on.

Gate. The Skirmiſh on both ſides waxed great , whott, and biolent. The egernes of our men, wrought the confuſion of as many as were then ſlayne . For if they had in tyme retyred, we had grǣued greatly the Enemy, without the loſſe of one man . For at the ſame preſent , we loſt many a proper Souldiar and tall gentleman The principall whereof, was Captayne Corne, Lieutenant Carie, Maiſter Browne, ſometimes a towardly and earneſt ſtudent of the Lawes in Lincoles Inne.

Blandy. Is this the Corne you ſpake of before?

Gate. The very ſame.

Blandy. I would her maieſty our moſt gracious Quéene and gouernour had all the empty barnes in England at this preſent, and boyde houſes full of ſuche Corne, as he was.

Gate. I do wiſh no leſſe.

Blandy. What of Lieuetenaunt Cary?

Gate. Cary appꝛoued in himſelfe euery way to come of a gentle and noble race, he had to his manlyneſſe, ioyned a ſinguler myldeneſſe and curteſy.

Blandy. What of Browne?

Gate. The lacke of experience was not in him ſo much lamentable, as value, fierceneſſe, and courage laudable.

Blandy. Were there ſlayne onely theſe at that pꝛeſent?

Gate. There were other in that confliœ conſumed, whoſe pꝛowes and ſtoutneſſe of right are pꝛayſewoꝛthy.

Blandy. Can you name them?

Gate. Some I know right wel, whoſe names were theſe, Williams, Snow, both bearing the office of a Corporall, Waller, a gentleman of the rounde, Brogdayne a pꝛiuate but a ſtout and couragious ſouldiar, one alſo I call to memoꝛy beſides, a man ỹ deſerued greatly & would (if life had laſted) haue pꝛoued an expert ſouldiar, his name was Samuell Gréene, with many moe, whoſe pꝛowes I comméd to thoſe, to whome theyꝛ pꝛoper names and peculiar natures are knowne as well, as to vs theyꝛ ſinguler manhood and rare bertue.

Blandy. What became of the enemy? was not his body in any part and member wounded?

Gate. Yes moſt déeply as you ſhall pꝛeſently vnderſtád. Foꝛ one halfe hower after this heate and bloudy bickeryng we being retyꝛed, immediately Roger Williams Captaine of the Engliſh hoꝛſemen, finding here and there dead carcaſes couering the playne, part of whoſe Coates and pꝛiuye marckes gaue him to thinke they were of his nation, ſpecially ſéeing the enemy neare vnto him, withoꝛew his Corownet of hoꝛſemé vnder the nuke of a mountayne, vttering bꝛiefly this maner of language. Gentlemen and fellow ſouldiars, we ſhall pꝛeſently pꝛoue the fauour of foꝛtune. Our lóg deſire hath bene to ſée the face of the enemy. My deare and louing countrey men behold now where the

body

body is . It is farr moɀe honoɀable foɀ vs to charge them in
this maner,then ſcattered, ſtraggeling, oɀ in Ambuſh and
Troupe,let this liuely ſight of dead bodyes, let freſh bloud
newly ſpilt,ſtirr and pɀicke you foɀwardes,let deſire of reuenge and victoɀy,lift vp your mindes,confyɀme your courage in my baloɀ and conſtancy : which(by that ſunne that
ſhineth and his gouernour I ſweare) ſhall not ſhɀinke and
quaile in this purpoſe intended . This ſayd, he himſelfe
firſt with the reſt of his gentlemen charged, and recharged
to the great loſſe of the enemy. He in that conflict ſlew one
hundɀed of the enemies folckes : Wonne two Enſignes,
bɀought away twenty ſeruiceable hoɀſes. Who comming
the next moɀning to the Campe was ioyfully receiued of
the General, Corownelles,Captaynes and Souldiars.

Blandy. His deſert required no leſſe , if his exployte be
well examined: wherein I know not whether I may commend moɀe his hardineſſe and value, (which hath bene alwayes thɀoughly appɀoued)oɀ happ and vertue , which in
a leader is as highly pɀiced , as neceſſarily reſpected . Foɀ
as it auayleth greatly an Armie to haue a happy Generall
ſo it incourageth not a litle any company on hoɀſe , oɀ foote
to be guided and lead by a foɀtunate commaunder , whiche
commeth not (as ſome thinke) by chaunce and of no certayne and pɀincipall cauſe,but rather (as I ſuppoſe) of a
ſuddayne and ſecret inſtinct and notice , that ſome man
hath aboue another:in perill to eſcape , in place to purſue,
in neceſſity to ſtand faſt, in doubt to be quickly and pɀudet-
ly reſolued , all which pɀocéede of a pɀoper and pɀiuy cir-
cumſpection of minde , which rare and excellent condition
and quality I yelde to this Captayne.

Gate. You haue yelded to him no moɀe then he may by
due challenge.

Blandy. Whereas Captayne Williams gaue the Enemy
a ſoɀe and ſharpe blow (wherein his true value eminently
appeared)there were other alſo no doubt,which did winne

at that pꝛeſent if not the like , yet great pꝛayſe and honoꝛ: in ſo much J verely think the meaneſt man, knowne leaſt foꝛ his triall and pꝛoofe,could not then but deſerue well. A⸗ mong echone Captayne Carelell now Serieant maior of the Engliſh Regiment , Criſtopher Champernoone the Gitternebearer, Browne a gentleman experte in riding, George Strawbrudge, Thomas Smith, Brooke, Argell, Thomſon, Turnor Lieuetenaunt befoꝛe of a Companp of footmē were mounted bꝛauely wᵗ many other. Theſe are to you well knowen, all whoſe pꝛiuate vertues as it is not in you to explayne , ſo if you will to pour ability diſcloſe any one ſpeciall pꝛopertp wherein they doe excell, and map (if it pleaſe God) they ſafe returne, be therefoꝛe wel imploy⸗ ed to theyꝛ Pꝛince & countrpes good , you ſhall bp pelding thē a moyetp of theyꝛ deſert, awake other of theyꝛ bloud & familiaritp here in England that be a ſlæpe: and thereby happelp winne them bp all honoꝛable meanes to ennoble theyꝛ names with the like exploytes and aduētures. What chieflp note you woꝛthp of pꝛapſe in Captayne Care⸗ lell, what in Champernoone, what in Browne the Rider, what in Strawbrudge, what in the reſt?

Gate. Captayne Carelell now Serieant Maior in fea⸗ ture and limmes of body is ſomething inferioꝛ to Captain Corne when he liued in pꝛopoꝛtion of minde, if you rſpect therein pꝛowes, equall: if pollicy, attapned bp learning and ſtudp, his ſuperioꝛ farre. Theſe two pꝛincipall giftes of a noble minde are in this Carelel beautiſied with other two in kinde and nature not ſo excellent, pet moſt ſit and neceſ⸗ ſarp to be reſident there , where true nobilitp pleaſeth to harbour.

Blandy. What are thoſe?

Gate. Affabilitp & liberalitp. Champernoone hath his va⸗ lue: moꝛe Græne, pet likely to be ripe and pꝛoue good fruit. Browne accoꝛding to his name is moꝛe then Græne, har⸗ dened thꝛough the pꝛoofe of many perilous attempt, whoſe

value

value , courage and fury , the enemy in this conflict felt,
through they fall and flight . Strawbrudge is a man of
finguler vertue and ſtoutneſſe . Doylye , Smith , Argell ,
Brooke , Thófon with ẏ reſt deſerue highly to be praysed.
Blandy. Shew (I pray you farther) your purpoſe intended.

Gate. After which conflict the Malecontentes could neuer
abide to encounter with ẏ Engliſh companyes,ſending to
Graue van Hollocke then Generall of the Army this pre
ty ieſt: Diſmiſſe Engliſh broode with they great Ruffes,
we care not a pinne for all thy Muffes . The malecontéts
therefore wandered through feare of Engliſh force as Pilgrims in they owne country hither and thither, accor ding
as they were informed by they ſpyes where the Engliſh
Regiment lay : promiſing many times to fight with vs,
meaning nothing leſſe , as the effect did proue. In meane
ſeaſon Mayſter Norris was made Generall of the whole
Army,not without his great deſert and triall of honor , by
whoſe vertue and pollicy the enemy of late hath bene ſo
plagued,that almoſt it is incredible to tell.

Blandy. I pray you vtter briefly the trueth thereof.

Gate. On Sonday before Chriſtmas laſt paſt 4. hundred
fifty and foure Malecontents were ſlayne by the Egliſhe
nation , at Swarfe Sluce in the weſt partes of Friſeland,
onely,with the loſſe of one Captayne named Elles & three
other priuate ſouldiars . The glory of which ouerthrow
and victory is chiefly to be geuen to God , the honor to M.
Norris and his Captaynes,the prayſe and commendation
to his officers and ſouldiars . In conſideration whereof, I
call to minde a prouerbe not ſo olde as true:As the king is
ſo is his people: which I may moſt fitly & truely apply to
M.Norris now Generall of the Armye of the States in
Friſeláð.As the Generall is , ſo are his Captaynes Lieue-
tenauntes,officers and ſouldiars . For where the deſire of
true honor,& glory is in the Generall imprinted, there the

H. i.   Captaynes,

Captaynes, officers, and souldiars, by a naturall loue and inclination that the best mindes are stirred therewith, are much moʒe set on fire and enkindeled.

So that whereas this noble gentleman, hath by his baliant actes, pʒoued himselfe to be a fountayne of fame, a welspring of vertue, a riuer of royaltye, it cannot be, but that his people become péerelesse, noble, and magnificent. Foʒ where the Generall féedeth his minde, with high and honoʒable causes, and standes therein resolute, there his Captaynes and Souldiars are pʒest to all manner of attemptes, be they neuer so difficult: And where such Captaynes are pʒest, there are atchiued feates moʒe wonderfull, then reasonable. And to speake something of our Nation, and especially, of the small and litle troupe vnder Maister Noʒris, it is incredible to thinke and repoʒt how their vertue doubleth the woʒthynes of other Nations. Foʒ as their leaders, and commaunders excell in witt, pʒowes, and value: so haue they them in moʒe loue, reuerence, and admiration. Foʒ this may be truely sayd of our Countrymen: that euen the rude multitude, doe loue their rulers, and superioʒs, accoʒding to their vertues, and magnanimitye, that they sée in them. No people in the woʒld moʒe faythfull, moʒe affectionate, then are the English Nation, if they be reteyned accoʒdingly: neither are they euercome a whitt with the hellish furies, and bʒutish crueltyes, that doe generally possesse all other Nations in the woʒld. Foʒ, it is naturally geuē to the right Englishman, to content himselfe with the victoʒy, and to take pittye on the banquished. And where this vertue of commiseration and mercye dwelleth, there also dwelleth naturally hardynes ⁊ pʒowes. Foʒ it is an infallible rule, that where feare is, there is also crueltye. So that I conclude of this pʒinciple: sith our Nation doth excell other in loue, gentlenes, courtesie, placabilitye and mercye, they also are to be pʒeferred befoʒe the straunger in true value, hardynes,

courage,

courage, p2owes, and magnanimitye.

Blandy. The ouerth2owe you fpeake of, was great : the p2ayfes and hono2 you haue geuen to Maiſter Norris is fuch, that he may in right challenge them. The commendation of our Countrye, you haue moſt firmely grounded on a fure rock of reafon. And whereas you haue made mé tion of the Generall, touching his fmall and litle troupe, to finiſh this wo2ke, in my opinion ſhall fitt you beſt, to geue all Gentlemen, and Souldiars of our Bation a farewell, who to winne their P2ince and Countrye hono2, feare no fo2ce, d2ead no daunger and terro2 of the Enemy. The number whereof, when J call to minde, J cannot forget Maiſter Iohn Seintleger: whofe value and p2owes ioyned with a p2incely humanitye and curtefie, my penn cannot deferuedly defcribe.

Gate. You haue J affure you, named a Gentleman: whofe valo2 matcheth with the vertue of the beſt of our nation, that ferue in the Bether Landes, although he be not a lyke p2eferred of the P2ince there: But no doubt if he indure thofe feruices he cannot but beare a p2incipall office, and that right wo2thelye in the field. His carefull payne in all exploytes, his equall labo2s in the ty?efome Barch, his d2eadles attemptes in any perilous aduenture haue bene fuch, fo open, and manifeſt, that not onely his Country men, but Souldiars of other nations, yelded him as his owne right, emong them bnknowen, a fuperio2itye. All which, Captayne Morris (a man of great experience and knowledge in feates of warre) can witnes. And whereas you haue occafioned me to fpeake fomething of Maiſter Seintleger (whome in this maner, J commend and commit to good fo2tune) you haue minded me of a Gentleman, who if he were no Gentleman by by2th and lynage, as he is well bo2ne, & of gentle bloud, yet he hath layed fo2 his name perpetually a foundatiõ, of high, and true Bobilitie.

Blandy. What is his name?

          H. y.   Gatc.

Gate. Rowland Yorke.

Blandy. The fame of his wifedome, and déepe aduife hath made me moꝛe inflamed with his perfon, then any foꝛmer and pꝛiuate knowledge.

Gate. What is the repoꝛt of him?

Blan. He is, fayth all that know the man (which cannot be fewe in number) bolde of courage, pꝛouident in direction, induſtrious in labour, and quick in execution.

Gate. What can be moꝛe defired in a Generall of an Armye?

Blandy. I referr that to the iudgement of other, but this I may well fay, that thefe are the moſt pꝛincipall poyntes which are to be required in a Gouernour. What think you of the other Captaynes of our Pation?

Gate. I finde Captayne Gaynſlord foꝛeward in the field, pꝛudent, liberall, and full of pollicye. Captayne Sallifbury fufficient, Captayne Byſhopp fure and ſtedfaſt, Captayne Richardes a pꝛoper and tall Souldiar, Captayne Bowes moſt fufficient.

Blandy. What of Liuetenaunt Senis? Liuetenant Forder, Liuetenant Fewilliams, Liuetenant Burley, Liuetenant Gittens, Liuetenant Haruye, Liuetenant Kelly?

Gate. Senis is expert, paynefull, louing, and courteous. Forder, baliant and foꝛtunate, Fewilliams redie, and refolute, Burley hautye, Gittens ſtoute, Haruie hardye, Kelly well appꝛoued.

Blandy. What of Auncient Manning? Auncient Marchant, Auncient Ling, Auncient Maſkrall, Auncient Bines.

Gate. All thefe are thꝛough long friall and experience ripe, moſt fitt to doe their countrye feruice.

Blandy. What thinke you of Dorrell, Leye, and Louelace.

Gate. Dorrell hath well deferued, Leye, if you looke into him thꝛoughly, may be iudged a man moſt fitt to take a charge, Louelace is not behinde the beſt of his oꝛder. which

are

are accompteo of.

Blandy. What of Knight, Baker, Cranmer, Coplwydge, Gray, Sallisburies both?

Gate. Knight, for his manlynes and actiuitye, for his strength and knowledge in euery weapon that belonges to a tall and expert Souldiar, may garde in peace and warre the Maieftye of an Emperor. The other haue by their de¬ fartes wonne fame and glorye.

Blandy. What of Smith, Owen, Padmore, Shepheard, Simmes, Rogers, Welch, with fiue hundred mo?

Gate. God, and well trayned Souldiars, all which, fo conftant is their courage, fo rare and refolute their mindes, fo flaming their fayth and fidelitye, long fithens bowed and confecrated to their prince and Countrey, that for her ma¬ ieftics fafetye, honor and fecuritye, they will at once moft readily and willingly adventure with Vliffes his wan¬ dringes, and doubtfull biages, fixe hundred fhippwrackes, the great glofe, and fwallowing fourge of Caribdis, the roaring of Silla, the daunger in auoyding the Antiphates, the greuous conflict which he had with Polephemus: fill vp with Curtius the gaping and daungerous breach: Per¬ forme in action, pouerty, lacke, and perill, although per¬ cafe not with the like happy happe with Drake the vnac¬ quaynted paffage and fteepe downe ftraightes of Maielan.

Blandy. More perfection in any people cannot be required. Wherfore I commend them all to good happ wifhing them (as naturall loue bindes me) a fafe and profperous return hither agayne, if not, that fruit and fucceffe of life which be¬ longes vnto thefe mindes which retayne true and perfect Nobility.

Gate. It appeareth therefore by your difcourfe that in a perfect commonwealth one chiefly fhould rule and fitt in the place of maiefty, other (chofen efpecially for their ver¬ tue, iuftice, prudence and pollicy) occupy a place of honour, by whofe wifedome and pollicy the multitude fhould be
H.iij.   gouerned

gouerned other some,foz theyz skill and vertue in warlike
pzactises be aduaũced to high degrée. Now J thinke it most
fit you speake of the Marchaunt,artificer,and Tiller of the
ground.

Blandy. When J consider with my selfe, how requisite and
necessary it is,that men should differ in degrée and dignity,
and that inumerable artes and sciences haue bene deuised
to mayntayne the common society of men,and no one may
excell in all, and few at any time may attayne the best : J
can no lesse maruayle at, then commend the deuine decrée
of nature, whose pzouidence hath wzought and appoynted
the barietyes of wittes,dispositions,& qualityes. Socrates
in his booke intituled Phedro calleth this excellency of nature ,the golde of the Gods, wherby he is induced to think
that they whose mindes are of so rare and fine a making,
are vnto them allyed and fitte of all other to be placed on
the earth in the Throne of Maiesty . Dame nature therefoze the mother of all thinges hath placed in the wozld pzin-
cipally such in the highest Roomes:of which ozder are kings
and Pzinces . Other some she hath not framed in such perfect wise,foz the clearnesse and shining glozy of vertue and
nobility:yet she hath imparted vnto them a most sharp wit
and ready capacity , greate balue and singuler pzouidéce.
Herehéce the iusticer and souldiar spzingeth , of which thzée
lofty and stately partes it is already discoursed . On other
she hath bestowed a mind and courage, that foz the magnificence of theyz pzince, weale of theyz countrey , honoz of
theyz City, estimation and creditt of theyz owne pziuate
familyes, will,by land,be the perill neuer so great,by sea,
be the daũger neuer so déepe and difficult , with the hassard
of vnknowen goods & déepe expence of a rich pursse,aduen-
ture straũge and vntried bioges.Herehence ŷ famous companies of aduenturing Marchauntes floweth , which are
the Pzinces of all other which buy and sell wares . Other
she hath made moze simple of vnderstanding, moze colde
of

of courage,and therefoze iustly hath appoynted vnto them,
to toyle in seruile artes , of which sozt are they , whome we
terme artificers,men of occupation, Tillers of the grounde
with theyz helpers,poze,simple,and laboursome men.

Gate. What you haue sayd hitherto of these thzæ partes
J can in no wise discommend.

Blandy. May not these suffice?

Gate. J am not vnacquaynted with your accustomed flo-
rishes,J know and am assuredly perswaded,you can if you
will and please deliuer moze of this matter.

Blandy. Will you that J wzite moze then J haue spoken?
Would you me attempt the commendation of theyz state?
If so,J shall hardly auoyd the suspitiõ of feare, oz flattery:
acknowledging notwithstanding how vnable a man J am
to yelde to the good and vertuous Marchaũt the true guerdon of his due desert.Would you me instruct them in theyz
kinde of life? Should my pen pinch oz impzoue their daynty fare?Should J be so bolde , as to enter into theyz house-
chappell, and mangle theyz to to much carued Imagery,
nipp theyz softe nice nightbeds? J assure you it is not my
part so to do.And albeit these(as some will)superfluities of
fend moze others that want such furniture , then in right
turne to the Marchauntes rebuke , being bought and pur-
chased with his paynefull & perillous trauayle : So no mã
of wise and dæpe iudgement shall be caried away from the
good opinion of a Marchaunt , thzough the sight of those
beautifull,pleasing,and passing vanities. If the Plowman
hath foz a shozt iozney at his seasan his swæte , if the laboz-
some man foz his dayly toile his penny,if the shepheard foz
his carefull care his pipe:much moze is it to be graunted to
ÿ Marchaunt,whose endeuozs are farre greater,whose tra-
uaile moze large,whose paines moze perillous,& full of er-
pence,his choise and solace , his rest and content at home,
and in his pziuate Family . All these pleasures are to him
graunted,if he perfozme what is in him required.

The Caftle of Pollicye.

Gate. What is his duety, and wherein chiefly doth it con-
fiſt?

Blandy. What I ſpeake is generall, and toucheth princi-
pally thoſe who haue wonne by any knde of foztune great
wealth, & yet ſtriue moſt egerly to augment ŷ ſame. I could
wiſh ſuch (as it becommeth Marchauntes indæd) to make
their marte wiſely wt ſtraungers in fozraigne landes, & not
to make a pzay wyly of the wantes of Gentlemen in theyz
owne countrye, what maketh the ſtate of any commonwealth moze flozishing thē aboũdance? Then, what plague
is found to the happyneſſe thereof moze peſtiferous, then
want & penury? If ſo, the pzocurers of the one are to be dete
ſted as much, as ŷ actozs of ŷ other right wozthely honozed.
And herein I pzay you note, that the Marchaunt whatſoeuer, which harkeneth after the wants, phantaſies, ſpending
humozs of gentlemen of his owne countrey, and eſpecially of ſuch who do kæpe good and wozſhipfull familyes, oz
of ſuch whoſe poſſeſſions thzough theyz Fathers vntimely
death, are come vnto them in the rage and fury of youth,
with an earneſt purpoſe and intention to chaunge launes
foz landes, gummy ſilcke foz a ſwæt and fat farme (abuſing
herein notwithſtanding theyz owne calling) geue theyz
Countrye to often moſt vnnaturally a dæpe and deadlye
wound.

Gate. Verely I thinke no leſſe. Is there any of ſo vile and
cozrupt minde in England?

Blandy. I can accuſe none: But if there be any, and
that my iudgemēt might be taken and accepted of, I would
haue all ſuch ſeared in the fozehead, with the marke, and
figure of death: ſignifyng therby, that whereas to this day
there is no lawe made, foz the inquiſition and puniſhing
here on earth, of ſo fowle and vnſatiable deſiers, there hath
bene from the beginning of the wozld, by the iuſt iudgement of God, appoynted a death in Hell: where ſuch ma-
lefactozs ſhall burne, and be tozmented with euerlaſting.

and

and vnquenchable fiers.

Gate. My buſines may not ſuffer me to ſtay long: Wherefore, proceede to the Artificer, and Tyller of the ground.

Blandy. All of one nature , are not indued with the ſelfe-ſame qualitye and vertue, neither is this difference to be noted in men onely: but in beaſtes, trees, and plantes. For trees which are of one kinde , ſpread not their braunches in lyke fayrenes, euery Stead doth not his Carrier with the lyke loftynes , neither is euery Lyon of lyke ſtregth. In all the workes of Nature, as I haue before declared , there is to be noted a varietye of value, diſpoſition , and qualitye : ſo that according to that diuerſitye , and inclina-tion of nature wee ſee the oddes of labors , and ſtud-dye. Some therefore according to their ſkill, and reach, embrace a ſcience , which more ſtrengtheneth ,and ſtayeth the weaker partes of a Commonweale, then other : in which place, I putt the Clothyer, other worke on gold and ſiluer , other worke on Iron , other till the ground , other in this, or that ſcience, beſtow their carefull paynes : all to the profitt and commoditye of their natiue Countrye. In conſideratiō of whoſe diuers diſpoſitions, in one kinde and nature,this I iudge moſt worthy to be reported,reade, and remembred : that Nature by diſpoſing our affections, ſo diuerſly,brought to paſſe moſt prouidently , that man, who of all other creatures was ordayned to maintayne a ſocietye , ſhould be thereunto forced of neceſſitye. For the trauayle of each man thus differing, yeldeth to other that which by his owne inſtuſtrye, he could neuer attayne.

Gate. You haue generally made mention of many ſcien-ces : among them all, the knowledge and ſkill of clothing, ſeemeth moſt worthye to be diſputed of : for that it concer-neth y̆ maintenaunce of thouſandes , whoſe good and proſ-perous ſtate , yeldeth to their Prince, in peace pleaſure, in warre, no ſmall ſupply of men , to withſtand the force and

furye

surye of the Enemye.

Blandy. I assent most gladly, to your good and honest desire, wishing my selfe as able, as willing, to vphold their state now falling, if the Prince, & prouidence of the Peeres and and nobilitye of England doe not with their pitifull eyes, and tender commiseration of so poore and approued condition of men, propp vp, and establish more strongly those thyghes, knees, and ioyntes of this Commonwealth.

Gate. Is the state of Clothiers infaebled?

Blandy. Their state is well nigh decayed, although they for the most part, retayne still their due, and naturall intention of minde, which causeth the to tast of some hardynes themselues, rather the nombers of good & honest me, (which cannot be otherwise relieue, the by their first learned occupation) should pearishe for want of sustenaunce.

Gate. In this action I assure you, they deserue much loue and reuerence. But how commeth it to passe, that men imployed in so good and honest trade of lyfe, should want the guerdon of so long and well approued toyle and labor?

Blandy. If you would know that, I thinke it most fitt, you sift, and search the ground and matter of their science.

Gate. What is that, they chiefely handle and worke on?

Blandy. Woll, Oyle, Dde, Madder, Gall, Ware, and many other thinges differing in nature, yet through the skill of y workema made one, all which, as they are not of one kinde, so are they not made, or ingendred in one place. Whose qualityes also differ greatly, and therefore, needeth the labor of many men to worke them, to the Artificers drift, vse, and knowledge. So that where there is a science in a commonwealth that handleth so many thinges, to the workemashipp whereof men in number are required, and besides where this faculty hath so long florished, being not stayned in any crime, that the Prince or commonwealth might conceiue griefe: I assure you (to speake the very trueth

trueth) the ouerthꝛow of clothmaking cannot but ouerthꝛow the body of a common wealth:except it be graunted
that a body may ſtand without legges . I could ſoꝛt this
ſcience into his bꝛaunches: that is,to the ſcience of making
narrow & bꝛoad clothes:ſetting downe by due compariſons
theyꝛ odds and peculiar difference.But foꝛ that I holde the
both of pꝛice,and that my pooꝛe and vnlearned penne may
litle pꝛeuayle them in this caſe,I refer them, and all other
cauſes whatſoeuer,to the Maieſty of God, whoſe vnſpeak-
able goodnes,vertue,& mercy I pꝛay , y̆ (whereas it hath
pleaſed him , y̆ all moꝛtall mē ſhould haue reaſō, although
not y̆ like capacity, all a minde,although not of like vnder-
ſtāding,y̆ all ſhould liue,although not in this woꝛld, in the
like ſtate, place,degrǽ, and dignity)it would pleaſe his diuine maieſty to graunt vs all in diſpoſition ſo differing, a
mind not differing,in inclination ſo much altering, the U-
nity of his ſpirit,grace,and vertue:the ineſtimable excellē-
cy wherof,lyeth open(thꝛough earneſt and careful pꝛayer)
as well to the pooꝛe man as Pꝛince, to the ſimple,as Pꝛudent,to the weak, as mighty,to the man that hath ſcarſe to
nouriſh and féd his hungry nature,as to him that aboun-
deth with all daynty and ſuperfluous fare . Who doth not
know how bile all theſe woꝛdly thinges are,how moꝛtall,
how trāſitoꝛy,how ful of erroꝛ & contēptible vanity? Who
doth not finde in himſelfe beholding y̆ vncertainty of riches
the wauering condition of honoꝛ and humayne gloꝛy , the
paynted ſhew of kinred and nobility, laſtly the counterfait
and deceitfull Image of ſwét ſayd pleaſures,his minde &
and harts deſire to be ſatiſſied? If ſo,why ſhould we ſtriue
ſo egerly foꝛ thoſe thinges that woꝛke our annoy and
perpetuall harme? If ſo, why ſhould we not earneſtly purſue vertue which leadeth vs to the
life which ſhall euer endure?
FINIS.

William Blandy to the gentle and
Friendly Reader.

Hus haue you reade (my ſinguler &
louing Fried) a diſcourſe not truely with
witt and learning poliſhed, in either of
which, becauſe I labor of a great defect,
I am right hartely ſory: but yet meet and
conuenient for thee to peruſe and know, whether thou
be of a gentle or vngetle condition. I haue ſtudied herein more to profitt, then to pleaſe, wherefore if thou haſt
ſought in the reading hereof, lippwiſedome, I haue fay-
led thee: If thy peculier or comowealthes commodity, a
profitt may happely ariſe hereof. My deſire is, that my
good meaning be not conſtrued amiſſe, which if thou
of thy ſinguler gentleneſſe and curteſy graunt, I
haue obtayned the hier of my labor: and thereby, I ſhalbe incouraged to attempt the diſ-
conrſe of ſome other matter hereaf-
ter for thy vſe, of greater waight
and importance.

AT LONDON
Printed by Iohn Daye dwel-
ling ouer Alderſgate.
Anno. 1581.

Cum Priuilegio Regiæ Maieſtatis.

Date Due

Demco 38-297